Junk Drawer

CHEMISTRY

50 AWESOME Experiments | That Don't
Cost a Thing

Experiments

BOBBY MERCER

CHICAGO
REVIEW
PRESS

Copyright © 2016 by Bobby Mercer
First edition
Published by Chicago Review Press Incorporated
814 North Franklin Street
Chicago, Illinois 60610

ISBN 978-1-61373-179-6

Library of Congress Cataloging-in-Publication Data
Mercer, Bobby, 1961– author.
  Junk drawer chemistry : 50 awesome experiments that don't cost a thing / Bobby Mercer.
— First edition.
     pages cm
  Audience: Ages 9+
  Audience: Grades 4 to 6
  ISBN 978-1-61373-179-6 (trade paper)
  1. Chemistry—Experiments—Juvenile literature. 2. Science—Experiments—
Juvenile literature. I. Title.
  QD38.M47 2015
  540.78—dc23

                                                              2015011435

Cover design: Andrew Brozyna, AJB Design, Inc.
Interior design: Rattray Design
Photo credits: Bobby Mercer

Printed in the United States of America
5 4 3 2 1

To Kim Kessler, Mike Garity, Megan, and Kylie,
thanks for always being there

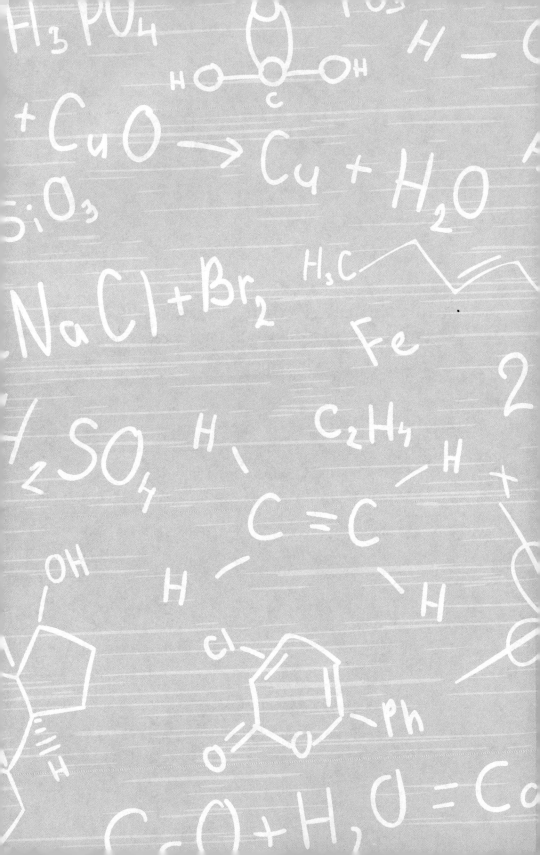

Contents

6 Radioactivity and Thermodynamics 169

Acknowledgments

Thanks to all the people who made this book series a reality. The teachers I work with truly inspire me on a daily basis and their insight is invaluable. Thanks to Laura Spinks, Jennifer Allsbrook, Sergey Zalevskiy, Kim Mirasola, Leslie Rhinehart, Lucas Link, and Shannon Haynes. Thanks to the best agent in the business, Kathy Green. Thanks to Jerome Pohlen, Amelia Estrich, and the creative people at Chicago Review Press for helping to shape this book. As always, I am eternally grateful to my wife, Michele, for allowing me and my assistants to make a mess in the name of science. And a special written shout-out to my two personal science assistants, Jordan and Nicole. Their tiny hands are featured in many of the photographs.

Introduction:
What Is Chemistry?

C hemistry is the science of how things around us interact. The natural laws that govern atoms, elements, and compounds are amazing. There are 92 natural elements. But from all these elements spring millions of compounds. For example, both diamonds and graphite (pencil lead) are pure carbon, but you can't do your homework with a diamond.

The heart of chemistry—the atom—is simple and, at the same time, complex. The easiest way to understand the atom is to think of the three basic parts that make up an atom: the proton, the neutron, and the electron. How those three parts combine and interact governs our world. Protons define what an atom is. Neutrons are the glue that holds atoms together. And the tiny electron is responsible for how molecules are formed, and it helps your hair stand on end with static electricity. And these subatomic particles are made up of even smaller parts, called quarks. However, this book will go no smaller than the three basic parts. But in the future, you may be the person who leads us into even smaller worlds.

\#   \#   \#

Science doesn't have to be expensive, but it should always be fun. The junk drawer is a great place to start learning about science. You might have to visit the kitchen or your bathroom for a few additional items, but most of the stuff needed for this book is already in your house. Turn all those things you have collected over the years into fun science experiments.

As a friend of mine says, **"Safety is your number one priority."** Read all the steps before proceeding. Get adult help when needed. Wear old clothes, tie up your hair, and wear sneakers when doing most of these experiments. All of these experiments are safe without safety goggles, but goggles do make you look more like a scientist.

Now it's time to learn about chemistry as you raid the junk drawer and all sorts of places around your house.

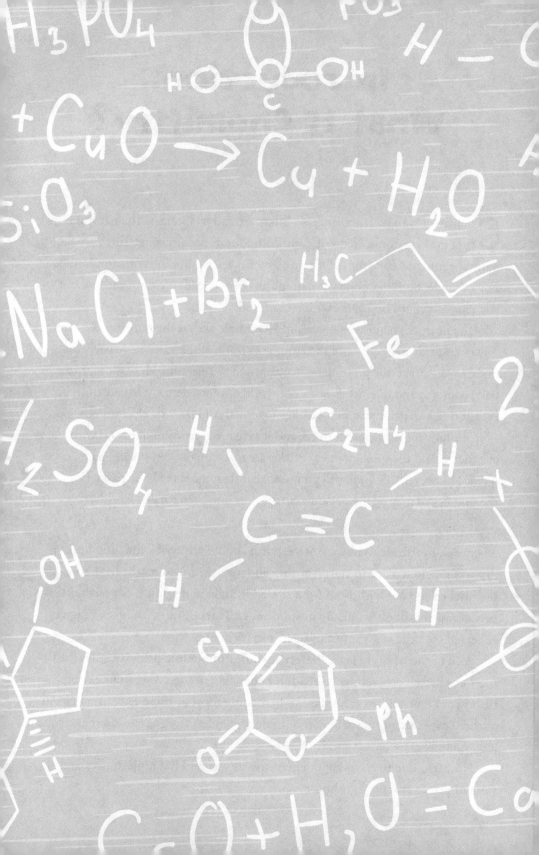

Properties of Matter

Matter is the stuff that makes everything around us. Everything you have touched, eaten, or played with in your life is probably composed of only 30 different elements. Elements are the basic building blocks of matter. We can put those elements together in so many different ways. Think of the plastic building blocks you probably played with as a kid. By putting them together in different ways you can create almost anything you desire. The simplest part of an element is the atom (more on the atom in chapter 2).

Let's jump in and learn some science about the world around us.

Can Can Dance

Watch two cans dance and learn about density.

From the Junk Drawer:
- ☐ Large sink (or glass aquarium, swimming pool, picnic cooler, or 2 large jars)
- ☐ Can of regular soda
- ☐ Can of diet soda

Step 1: Fill a large container with at least 8 inches of water. A kitchen sink is perfect. You can also use an aquarium (without fish in it), swimming pool, picnic cooler, or two large jars. Put an unopened can of diet soda and an unopened can of regular soda in the water. Observe what happens.

Step 2: Push the floating can under the water and observe. Share this experiment with your friends at your next party.

The Science Behind It

Objects float because of density. Density is mass divided by volume. Something with tightly packed atoms, like most metals, will have a high density. Loosely packed atoms, like the helium gas in a balloon, have a lower density. The easiest way to compare density is with water.

Water has a density of 1 gram per cubic centimeter (g/cm^3; a cm^3 is also called a milliliter). If an object floats, it has a density less than 1 gram per cubic centimeter. If it sinks, the density is greater than 1 gram per cubic centimeter. The diet soda has an overall density less than 1 gram per cubic centimeter, so it floats. Regular soda has a density greater than 1 gram per cubic centimeter, so it sinks.

What is the difference between the two sodas? Sugar (in all its forms) increases the density of the regular soda. Diet soda is sweetened with a chemical, and it only takes a tiny amount to create the same sweetness that sugar creates. Therefore, there is more matter in a can of regular soda than in a diet soda, making it denser.

In a swimming pool, you can change your body's density by breathing. You decrease your overall volume when you breathe out. Your density increases to more than 1 gram per cubic centimeter. You sink, but you will swim up pretty quickly because you need air. For more on floating, you can go to the chapter on solutions (page 85).

Air Is Heavy

Use two balloons to learn one of the secrets of matter.

From the Junk Drawer:

☐ 2 balloons
☐ 3 pieces of string, each about 6 inches long
☐ Clear tape
☐ Ruler
☐ Pin or sharp scissors

Step 1: Blow up two balloons to equal size and tie a knot in the neck of each balloon. Tie a string around each knot.

Step 2: Use tape to secure the string from each balloon to opposite ends of a ruler.

Step 3: Tie another length of string around the center of the ruler. Hang the center string from the edge of a table using tape. (You can actually hang it from anything as long as it hangs freely.) Slide the ruler through the center

string until it balances level. This is difficult and will take some practice. It does not have to be perfectly level, but it should be close.

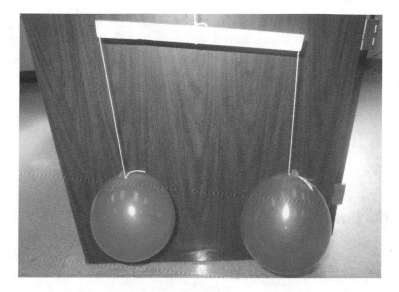

Step 4: Take a pin or a pair of sharp scissors and create a tiny hole near the neck of one of the balloons. The rubber is thicker near the neck so the balloon won't pop, but the air will slowly leak out. Observe what happens as one balloon deflates. Why do you think that happened?

The Science Behind It

Air is matter, and all matter has weight. As you saw from this experiment, a balloon full of air has more weight than an empty balloon. Blow up a balloon, tie it off, and let it go. It always falls because air, and the rubber balloon itself, both have weight. Balloons only float if they are filled with a lighter-than-air gas such as helium.

Three Balloons of Fun

Learn the secret to the states of matter with three balloons.

From the Junk Drawer:

☐ 3 balloons of equal size   ☐ Freezer
☐ Water

Step 1: Fill one balloon with air and tie a knot in it. Fill two more balloons with water and tie the balloons off. Try to make all the balloons close to the same size. Put one of the water-filled balloons in the freezer overnight (or for at least six hours). You want the freezer balloon to be completely frozen.

Step 2: A day later, take all three balloons outside. Squeeze each with your hands. What do you observe?

Step 3: Drop each balloon from about 1 foot above the ground. What do you observe?

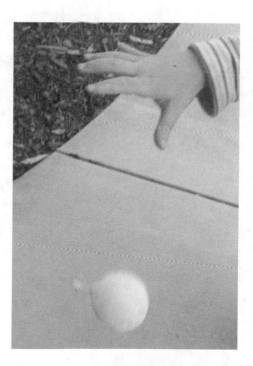

Step 4: Now throw them away from you as high as possible. What happens?

Step 5: If any of the balloons haven't popped, pop them now and observe what happens. How is the material in each balloon different?

The Science Behind It

All matter is composed of one of four states: solid, liquid, gas, or plasma. The gas balloon, filled with air, was almost impossible to pop by throwing or dropping. That is because of the wonders of a gas. Gases are lightweight, so this was the lightest balloon. Gases can also change shape and volume. For that reason, the balloon was squishy. That is the reason this balloon was the hardest to pop. When you popped the gas balloon, the gas immediately started spreading out and mixing with the other gases in the air around it. In summary, gases are lightweight and able to take any shape and volume.

The liquid-filled balloon popped more easily because liquids are heavier, but they still move. The liquid also was squishy, but it never changed its volume. When the liquid-filled balloon popped, the liquid came out and stayed flat on the ground. The liquid changed shape, but the volume stayed the same. In summary, liquids are heavier than gases and have a definite volume, but will take any shape possible.

The solid balloon was the heaviest. The solid-filled balloon was also difficult to break. The solid ice inside kept the same shape and volume all the time. In summary, solids are heavier and keep the same shape and volume. Your solid chunk of ice may break into pieces when you drop it or throw it. If it didn't already break the balloon, you can change its shape with a hammer. Go ahead—try it!

The fourth state of matter, plasma, is like a gas, but it has an electric charge. A fluorescent lightbulb is filled with a plasma. It is a gas that conducts electricity. Since it conducts electricity, it will create light when an electric charge is placed across it. The sun is a giant ball of plasma. To create a plasma it takes extreme heat, like the sun, or high amounts of electricity, like a plasma ball or a fluorescent lightbulb.

Homemade Stress Balls

Make super squishy fun balls with a few balloons.

Adult supervision required

From the Junk Drawer:

☐ Empty plastic drink bottle
☐ Serrated knife
☐ Oven mitt (recommended)
☐ Scissors

☐ 4 balloons of equal size
☐ Rice, flour, or salt
☐ Spoon or fork

Step 1: With adult permission or help, use a serrated knife to cut a slit in the side of an empty plastic drink bottle. For safety purposes, you could use an oven mitt to hold the bottle. You just need to puncture an opening in the bottle—you will use scissors to finish it.

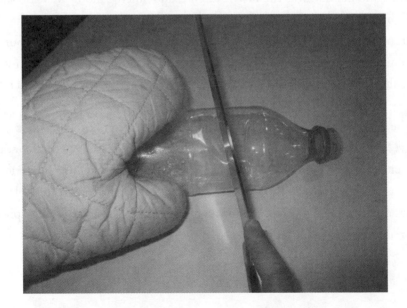

Step 2: Insert scissors into the opening and continue to cut around the bottle. This is a great way to create a homemade, wide-mouth funnel for any experiment.

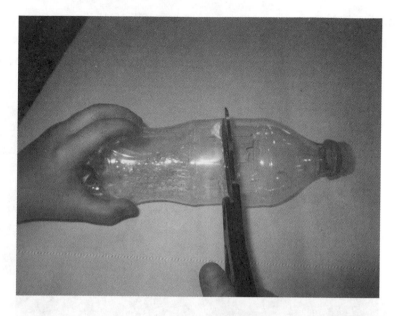

Step 3: Blow up a balloon and allow it to deflate. Do this again several times. This stretches out the balloon and makes it easier to fill later. Stretch the neck of the balloon over the top of the bottle. When you turn it upside down, the balloon should hang freely.

Step 4: To avoid making a mess, go outside to fill the balloon. Fill your funnel with rice. Flour or salt also works well. Shake the funnel to allow the rice to fall into the balloon. You can put your hand over the top to prevent the rice from shaking out the top of the funnel.

Step 5: Use the handle of a spoon or fork to push even more rice down into the balloon. Fill the balloon until you have a small round ball.

Step 6: Remove the balloon from the funnel. Use your hands to massage the ball to get all of the rice into the body of the balloon and to get rid of as much air as possible. Tie a knot in the balloon close to the body. Now go back inside to finish the rest.

Step 7: Use scissors to cut the part of the balloon beyond the knot. Cut very close to the knot *without* cutting the knot.

Step 8: Cut the neck off two other balloons.

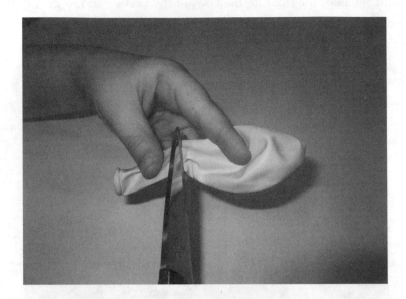

Step 9: With both hands, stretch out the body of one of the balloons. Have a friend or parent push the rice-filled ball into the stretched-out balloon. Put the knot in first to prevent any mess. Repeat with the other cut balloon. You should end up with a three-layer stress ball that won't leak.

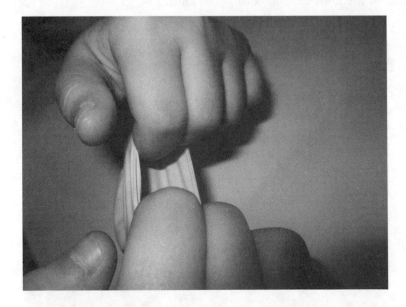

Step 10: Any good Stress Ball needs a stripe. Choose a contrasting color balloon and cut off the neck and the top.

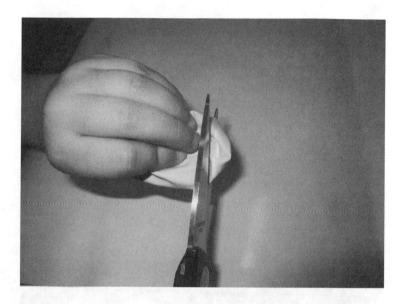

Step 11: Stretch the stripe around the center of the ball. Make sure it covers the opening from step 9.

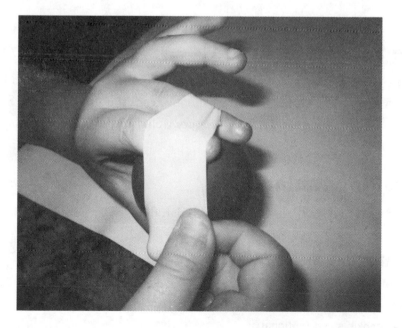

Step 12: Grab the ball and give it a good squeeze. Create three stress balls and teach yourself to juggle.

The Science Behind It

The rice (or whatever you used) acts like a very thick fluid. It moves and flows, just very slowly. The rubber from the balloons keeps the "liquid" inside. Since it acts like a liquid, the balls don't bounce very well. But they are fun to play with.

Non-Newtonian Goo

Make a mess and learn about non-Newtonian fluids at the same time.

From the Junk Drawer:

☐ Box of cornstarch   ☐ Water
☐ Large mixing bowl   ☐ Food coloring (optional)
☐ Large cookie sheet (optional)

Step 1: Empty an entire 16-ounce box of cornstarch into the mixing bowl. Cornstarch is very inexpensive, and this experiment might be the most fun you will ever have with a dollar. This experiment is best done outside on a picnic table, for easy cleanup. If you do it inside, you might want to put the bowl on a large cookie sheet.

Step 2: *Slowly* add water. Mix it with your hands. Of course, you can use a spoon, but hands are so much more fun. Add more water in small quantities until the mixture flows slowly, like a superthick liquid. Stop and play with it periodically; you can always add more water. You can add food coloring if you want to.

Step 3: Now pick up a handful of the goo and try to hold it. What happens after you lift it?

Step 4: Make a fist and punch it into the mixture. What happens?

Step 5: Now sink your finger into it slowly. Why do you think it behaves that way?

Step 6: Pour it from hand to hand. It will flow just like a liquid if you do it slowly.

Step 7: After you are done playing with the goo, go outside if you haven't already. Roll a handful of goo into a ball and try to bounce it on the sidewalk. With the right consistency, you can actually get it to bounce once. Of course, it will ooze into a liquid again after the first bounce. Clean up when you are done and share the joy of Non-Newtonian Goo with friends and family. This is a great experiment to do at an outside summer picnic. Dilute the mixture heavily with water as you pour it down your sink if you are inside; if you don't, you could end up with a plugged drain.

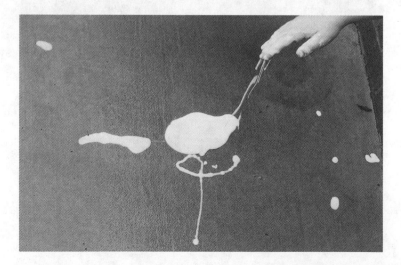

Optional Step 8: If you buy about 20 boxes of cornstarch, you can create enough of the cornstarch mixture that you can dance on it in bare feet. You would need a large tub, like a storage tub (*not* a bathtub), to do this. As long as you move your feet quickly, you can dance on it. Stop, and you sink.

The Science Behind It

Viscosity is the term used for friction between molecules of a liquid. Water has a low viscosity and flows easily. Heat it up and it flows more easily. Honey has a lot of viscosity if it is cold. But if you warm up honey, it will pour almost like water. These are called Newtonian fluids because Isaac Newton did a lot of research on viscosity. He found that the viscosity of most liquids depends on their temperature. The hotter the liquid, the less viscosity, so it flows more easily.

The cornstarch goo you created is a non-Newtonian fluid. The goo's viscosity increases in response to the force you apply to it or the speed at which an object moves through it. Punch it and you get high viscosity. Ketchup and Silly Putty are other examples of non-Newtonian fluids. Ketchup's viscosity decreases when you apply pressure to it. If you shake up the bottle, the ketchup will pour more easily.

Electric Water

Curve a stream of water to learn about water's amazing polar nature.

From the Junk Drawer:
☐ Water faucet
☐ Balloon

Step 1: Turn on a water faucet and adjust the flow until the stream is extremely thin. An interesting thing happens with water streams. When you look at a water stream with your eye, you see a solid stream most of the way down, but you can see it breaking into drops at the end. With a high-speed camera, you can actually see the drops appear at a much higher level. Use your parents' camera or a really good cell phone camera and prove it to yourself.

Step 2: Blow up a balloon and tie a knot in it. Now rub the balloon vigorously on your hair. You can also rub the balloon with any thick material, like a sock or a sweater. The fuzzier the better.

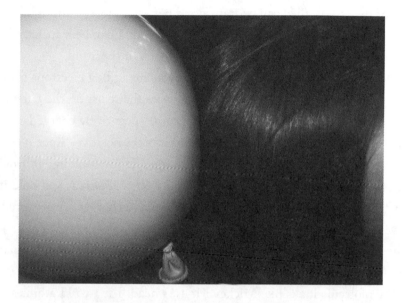

Step 3: Bring the balloon close to the stream of water. Keep moving it closer until you see the stream curve.

The Science Behind It

All items start out neutral. That means they have an equal number of positive charges (protons) and negative charges (electrons). Since electrons are on the outside of the atoms, they can be transferred between objects through contact. As a matter of fact, the electrons are the only part that can be transferred, since the protons are tightly held in the nucleus (center) of the atom.

When you rub the balloon on your hair, you are adding electrons from your hair. Electrons are the tiny negative particles that exist on the outside of an atom. The balloon gains electrons and becomes negatively charged on the side that was rubbed on your hair. Your hair becomes positive. Since it lost negative charges, it now has extra positive charges. If you look in a mirror, you will see that a few hairs will stretch out to touch the balloon as you hold it close after rubbing your hair. That is because positive charges are attracted to negative charges (and vice versa).

The stream of water bends toward the balloon because of water's polar nature. Water is composed of two hydrogen (H) atoms and one oxygen (O) atom; the molecule looks like Mickey Mouse's head. The two H atoms are small and form its ears, but the H atoms are also positive. The larger O atom forms the head and is negative. The overall water molecule is neutral but the bottom end is negative and the top (ear) end is positive.

The stream of water bends toward the balloon because the positive side of the water molecule is attracted to the negative side of the balloon. If you had a positively charged object near the stream of water, the water would also curve. It would curve because the other side of the Mickey Mouse head would be attracted to the positive object.

The Impossible-to-Blow-Up Balloon

Create a balloon that you can't blow up to learn about air and pressure.

From the Junk Drawer:
☐ Empty plastic bottle with a thin neck
☐ Balloon

Step 1: Push an empty balloon down into an empty plastic bottle. Keep the neck of the balloon outside of the bottle.

Step 2: Stretch the neck of the balloon over the rim of the plastic bottle.

Step 3: Now try to blow up the balloon inside the bottle. Try harder, but don't get too upset and don't hurt yourself trying. The title of the experiment says it all: you can't blow up the balloon inside the bottle!

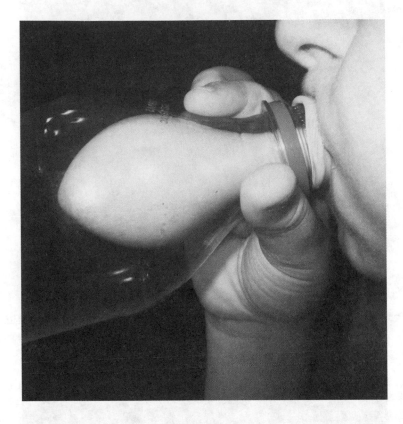

The Science Behind It

An empty bottle isn't really empty. It is full of air, and air takes up space. As you blow into the balloon, the air inside the bottle (but outside the balloon) is compressed and the balloon inflates slightly. But the air has no place to go, so the balloon will quickly stop inflating. The air inside the balloon has greater than normal air pressure from your lungs. The stronger your lungs are, the more the balloon will inflate, but it will never inflate completely.

To inflate the balloon in the bottle, try the next experiment.

The Impossible-to-Deflate Balloon

Learn more about air pressure as you create a balloon that won't deflate.

From the Junk Drawer:

☐ Balloon and bottle combination from the Impossible-to-Blow-Up Balloon experiment

☐ Thumbtack or pushpin

Step 1: Use a thumbtack or pushpin to poke a hole in the bottom of the plastic bottle. Wiggle the tack or pin around to make the hole larger.

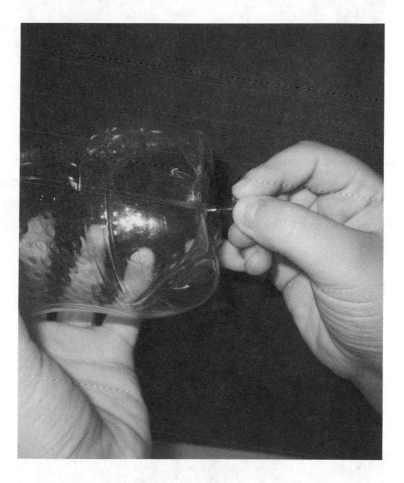

Step 2: Now blow up the balloon inside the bottle. It may take several breaths, but it will now inflate inside the bottle. (A larger thumbtack hole allows the balloon to inflate faster.) It probably will not completely fill the bottle. It will only inflate until the balloon securely touches the inside wall all the way around the balloon.

Step 3: Once the balloon is inflated, with your mouth still on the neck of the balloon, use your finger to cover the hole in the bottle tightly. You could also use a small piece of tape to block the hole. Keep the hole blocked as you remove your mouth. The balloon will stay inflated as long as the hole is plugged.

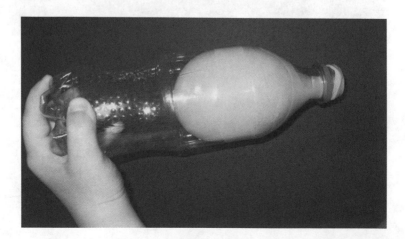

Step 4: Unplug the hole and watch the balloon deflate. You can repeat the experiment as many times as you want. If you plug the hole before you attempt to blow up the balloon, you will get the same result as the Impossible-to-Blow-Up Balloon.

The Science Behind It

The thumbtack hole gives the air in the bottle a way to escape. As the balloon inflates inside the bottle, the air in the bottle escapes out through the hole. Some air will probably be trapped near the mouth end of the bottle, but your lungs should be able to create enough air pressure to completely inflate the balloon inside the bottle.

As you blow up the balloon, the extra air pressure from your lungs causes the balloon to expand. When you plug the hole with the balloon inflated and remove your mouth, the trapped air pressure inside the balloon and inside the bottle (but outside the balloon) will be equal. You can actually inflate the balloon and keep it the same size at any time just by plugging the hole. Try it. Blow the balloon halfway up and plug the hole. Remove your mouth and watch the balloon. It will stay the same size.

Air always flows from high pressure to low pressure. If the pressure is the same, the air won't move significantly. It will move randomly back and forth through the opening to the balloon, but not enough will move to make the balloon change shape. That molecules of matter always move is one of the fundamental assumptions of science.

Pure gold is so soft you can bend it with your hand. Gold used in jewelry has had other metals added to it to make it stronger.

Mysterious Floating Paper Clip

Steel sinks in water . . . or does it?

From the Junk Drawer:

☐ Bowl
☐ Water
☐ 2 small paper clips
☐ Facial tissue

Step 1: Fill a bowl with water. Drop a paper clip into it. What happens? It sinks. Everyone knows steel sinks in water, right?

Step 2: Take a piece of facial tissue and fold it up until it fits inside the bowl. Gently lay a new paper clip on top of the tissue. Keep the tissue as flat as possible as you *gently* lay it on top of the water. Watch for a minute as the tissue paper absorbs water and sinks. The steel paper clip is now floating on the water. You can try it with larger paper clips, but it probably won't work. The small paper clips always work.

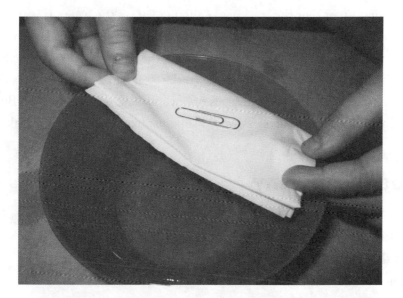

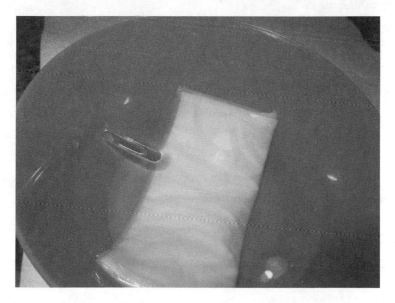

The Science Behind It

Water has surface tension because it is a polar molecule. Polar molecules have a positive end and a negative end. Since opposites attract, the positive ends stick to the negative ends and create a tough "skin" for the water. The tough skin is actually pretty strong—strong enough to support a steel paper clip if conditions are right.

It is important that the steel paper clip lies flat on the water. If you dropped it or if it goes in at an angle, the surface tension "skin" is not strong enough to help it float. As the tissue dissolves, the weight of the paper clip is spread out and the surface tension helps the steel paper clip float. It is this surface tension that allows some types of bugs to walk on top of water. But the insects have to be light. Big bugs would sink just like big paper clips sink.

Super Wet Penny

How wet can a penny get?

From the Junk Drawer:
☐ Penny
☐ Medicine dropper
☐ Water

Step 1: Lay a dry penny on a smooth, waterproof surface. Use a medicine dropper to add 10 drops of water to the surface of the penny. If you don't have a medicine dropper (or eye dropper), ask your parents if they have one in the medicine cabinet. Many children's medicines come with them. A baby syringe will also work and comes with many medicines. You can also use an empty bottle from eye drops or contact lens solution if you can rinse it and refill it with water. In a pinch, you can even use a straw. To use a straw, put the straw down in water and put your thumb over the end of the straw. When you lift the straw it will pick up water due to air pressure. By quickly removing and replacing your thumb, you can let out tiny amounts of water. However, the other methods are easier to control.

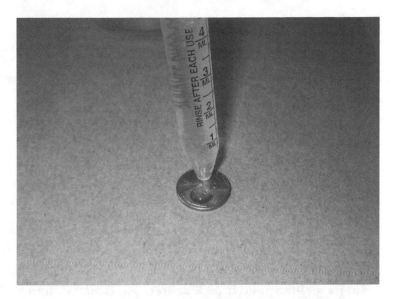

Step 2: Continue adding drops of water, one at a time, to the penny. Stop after about fifteen drops and look carefully at the water on the penny. Put your eye down at the level of the penny and you will see a water "bubble." Count the number of drops you can add until the water finally leaks off onto the surface. Does the number surprise you?

Extension: Try using other coins.

The Science Behind It

The number of drops you can put on a penny is amazingly large, if you are gentle. You have probably already guessed that surface tension is the cause of this phenomenon. And you are right. The penny also has a ridge around the edge from where it was stamped at the mint. The edge makes a great container for your water "bubble."

Gallium is a silver metal with a unique property:
it will melt in your hand. It is a solid at room temperature.
But its melting point is 85.6 degrees, so it melts when
in contact with your skin.

Scared Pepper

Send pepper racing away from itself.

From the Junk Drawer:
☐ Bowl
☐ Water
☐ Pepper
☐ Toothpick
☐ Liquid soap

Step 1: Fill a bowl with water. Sprinkle pepper across the top of the bowl. (This is a perfect use for the little paper pepper packets you get from restaurants, but a pepper shaker will also work.)

Step 2: Dip a toothpick through the surface of the water to the bottom of the bowl. What do you observe?

Step 3: Pull the toothpick out of the water. Now dip one end of the toothpick into some liquid soap. Put the soapy end of the toothpick into the water and watch what happens.

The Science Behind It

The pepper flakes will float on top of the water. Pepper is hydrophobic, meaning pepper is not attracted to water. Pepper, unlike salt, will never dissolve in water. The pepper floats on the "skin" of the water created by surface tension. Although the clean toothpick penetrates the water, it doesn't change the surface tension except right at the insertion point.

Since soap is a surfactant (short for surface acting agent), it decreases the surface tension. The soap enters from the toothpick point and quickly disrupts the surface tension. The water molecules try to keep the surface tension and run away from the soap. The floating pepper shows the water molecules running away from the soap.

Soap helps us clean by allowing water to lose some surface tension. That allows grease and oil, which make us dirty, to move more freely in the water. Molecules in the soap are designed to "suck up" the grease and oil. As you rinse off, the soap carries away the grease and oil, along with any dirt trapped in the grease and oil.

Mysterious Levitating Candle

Adult supervision required

From the Junk Drawer:

☐ Baking pan, dinner plate, or pie plate
☐ Water
☐ Tea light candle
☐ Matches
☐ Empty glass jar that fits over the candle

Step 1: Fill a baking pan (or dinner plate) with about ½ inch of water. Place a tea light candle in the water.

Step 2: Light the candle. Be careful to do this on a fireproof surface. Also, blow out the match and dip it in the water to completely cool it off.

Step 3: After the candle has been burning for about a minute, invert a glass jar and place it over the candle. Watch what happens.

The Science Behind It

The secret here is Charles's Law. Charles's Law says that volume and temperature are directly related. When temperature goes up, volume goes up. And when temperature goes down, volume goes down.

When the candle is burning, the hot gas above it expands. As you place the jar over the top of the candle, the oxygen in the jar will allow the candle to burn for a few seconds. After the candle goes out, the gas in the jar will rapidly cool down. As the gas cools down, the volume of gas goes down and the water rises. If the candle is floating, it will levitate with the water surface.

Shrunken Heads

Create your own crazy shrunken head from an empty chip bag.

Adult supervision required

From the Junk Drawer:

☐ Empty foil-lined snack-size   ☐ Large marker
   chip bag   ☐ Microwave oven
☐ Scissors   ☐ Plate

Step 1: Use scissors to cut off both ends of an empty snack-size chip bag.
Any bag that has a very thin silver lining inside will work. The experiment
is easy to do, so you could test other types of bags. Any size bags will work.
The bags shown below are individual snack-size bags. This is a fun activity
for a sleepover or a birthday party. Eat the chips and then have each person
create his or her own Shrunken Head to take home.

Step 2: Use scissors to cut along both sides of the bag. You will be left with two rectangles of the wrapper.

Step 3: Turn the shiny side up and wipe it clean of any crumbs or oil. Using a large marker, draw a face on your bag. The face needs to cover most of the bag. Smiley faces are easy to draw, but be creative.

Step 4: Place the bag (shiny side up) on a microwaveable plate and place it in the microwave oven. Microwave on high for **five seconds** only. **Do NOT microwave longer.** Watch it through the door of the microwave oven while you are doing it. You will see a spectacular light show, but it does not hurt the microwave oven. **Let the Shrunken Head cool for at least two minutes** before touching it.

Step 5: Repeat for the other half of the bag. Try a different picture or just write your name on the bag in large letters.

The Science Behind It

The bags are composed of polymers, which are long chain molecules. In the process of making the bag, putting chips in it, and sealing it, the polymers are straightened out. The polymers' natural shapes are bent and curled. When you microwave the bags, the polymers heat up and go back to their natural state, and the bag shrinks, along with anything you have drawn on it.

The light show you witnessed is created by the thin aluminum coating used in the bags. The microwaves cause electrons in the foil to move quickly back and forth. The electrons pile up on the sharp points of the bag. The air around the points becomes electrically charged and the electrons leave the bag as a spark. The sparks are small but noticeable. This is completely safe as long as it is done for only a short time and you have nothing that can catch fire inside the microwave, like a paper towel or paper plate.

Wriggling Wrapper Snake

Make a snake come alive in the name of science.

From the Junk Drawer:

☐ Paper-wrapped drinking straw

☐ Cookie sheet or baking tray (optional)

☐ Water in a cup or glass

Step 1: Hold a paper-wrapped drinking straw upright on a tabletop with one hand. Push the wrapping paper down the straw with the other hand.

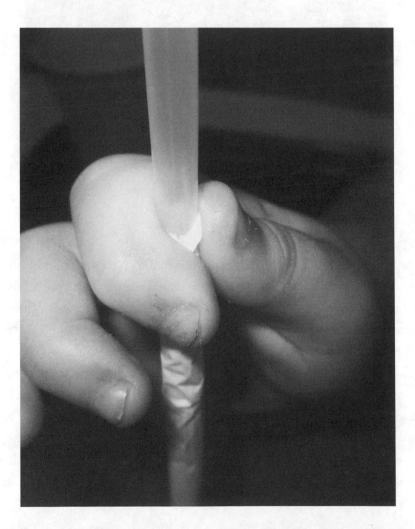

Step 2: Continue pushing the wrapper all the way down the straw. Try to bunch all of the paper together as you push it down the straw.

Step 3: Place the scrunched-up wrapper on a tabletop or countertop. Make sure the tabletop is one that can get wet since we will add water in the next step. A cookie sheet or baking tray works well if you are worried about water on your table.

Step 4: Put the straw in your water and place your finger (or thumb) over the top of the straw. This will trap water inside the straw for the next step.

Step 5: Remove your finger and replace it quickly. This will let only a few drops of water out. If you have never done this before, practice a few times before you make the Wrapper Snake. Now let a few drops of water fall onto one end of the Wrapper Snake. Watch it grow. Repeat for any parts of the Wrapper Snake that are dry until it has grown to its full length.

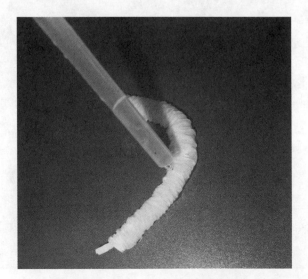

The Science Behind It

My best friend, Matt, has entertained my daughters for years with this trick every time we have gone out to eat. It is a perfect way to entertain your family as you wait for food.

Paper is made of very tiny wood fibers. When you scrunch it up, these fibers compress. As the water soaks into the paper straw wrapper, the paper swells and the tiny fibers straighten out. Your Wrapper Snake grows as this happens. Let's use the same process to make a dancing snake.

Frogs don't need to drink water. They can absorb it right through their skin.

Snake-Charmed Dancing Wrapper

Use science to make your snake dance.

From the Junk Drawer:

☐ Paper-wrapped drinking straw   ☐ Water in a cup or glass

Step 1: Tear off one end of the paper wrapper and slide the drinking straw out. You want the long, empty paper wrapper for this project.

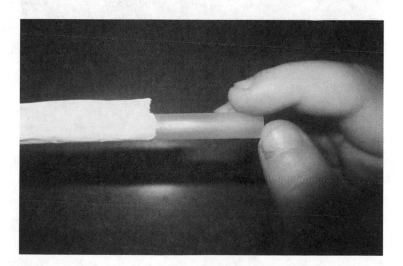

Step 2: Twist one end of the paper wrapper as tightly as possible. Be careful not to rip the paper wrapper.

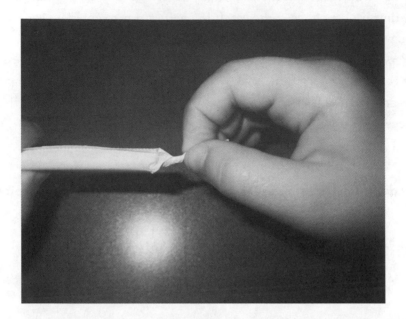

Step 3: Continue twisting until the entire wrapper is twisted up very tightly.

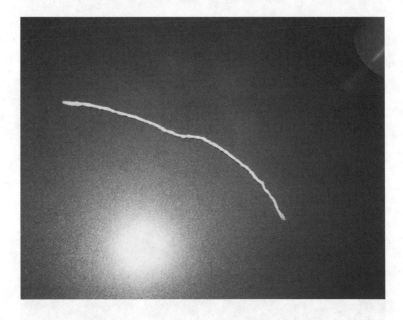

Step 4: Put the straw in water and place your thumb (or finger) over the top
to trap water. Put a few drops of water at one end of the Snake-Charmed
Dancing Wrapper and watch what happens. Try it again and experiment
with where to put the water and how much to use. Share the Snake-
Charmed Dancing Wrapper with your family and friends the next time
you go out to eat.

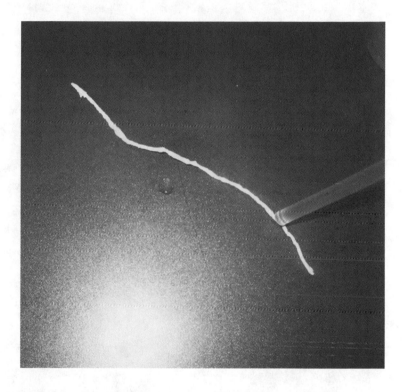

The Science Behind It

In many countries, snake charmers get snakes to dance with rhythmic music
and movement. You get to use chemistry to make your wrapper dance. The
fibers of the paper are twisted up by you. As water is absorbed into the wrapper, the fibers want to straighten out like they were before. Since they are
twisted, they untwist as they straighten. This untwisting action causes the
Snake-Charmed Dancing Wrapper to dance on your tabletop.

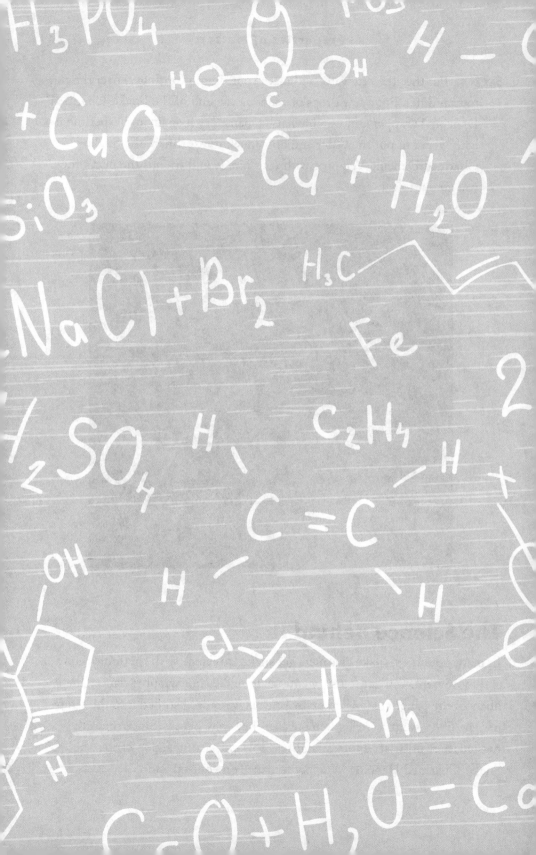

Atoms, Compounds, Elements, and the Periodic Table

The heart of chemistry is the atom. Atoms make up the elements that govern the world around us. Atoms are tiny. We will never see inside one, but we can still understand how they work. How they work and how they combine affects everything—food, clothing, and toys . . . even how we breathe and digest.

You will learn a little about how scientists can observe things they can't see. You will also see how scientists created the roster of elements that chemists call the periodic table. You will even learn how atoms can combine to form new compounds. A compound is just a combination of atoms, like water, which is a combination of two hydrogen atoms and one oxygen atom—two gases that combine to form that fabulous liquid that keeps us alive.

Now it's your turn to experiment and study the atom.

Black Box

Use a marble to learn how scientists model an atom that is too small to see.

From the Junk Drawer:

☐ Various small shapes like blocks, paper clip boxes, plastic thumbtack boxes, etc.

☐ Large piece of plain paper (or newspaper)

☐ Shoe box lid

☐ Friend, sibling, or parent

☐ Marble

☐ Pen, pencil, or marker

Step 1: You are going to discover how to create a model of something you can't see, so a partner is a must for this experiment. If you construct it, you will know the secret, so close your eyes or leave the room while your partner places a single object on top of the large piece of paper. Tall objects work best, since you want the edges of the box lid to be suspended above the paper. In class, I use large paper clip boxes, but blocks of wood also work well. Large tuna fish cans work well for round objects. This is also a great use for repurposing old newspaper. If you draw on it with a marker, the marks will be visible even with the printing on the paper. In class, we always use newspaper, since it is free and easy to recycle. The photos below were taken with four pieces of plain white paper taped together to make the steps easier to see.

Step 2: Have your partner place the shoe box lid over the top so you can't see the object. Now you can open your eyes or come back into the room.

Step 3: Roll the marble under the shoe box lid. Roll it hard enough that it comes back out, either after bouncing off the shape or after rolling straight through. Flicking it with your finger usually works well. Be careful to look straight down at the top of the shoe box lid. The goal is to create a model of something you *can't* see—no peeking.

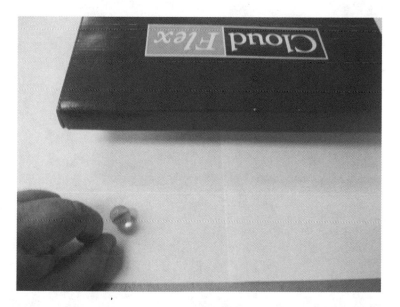

Step 4: Using a marker, pen, or pencil, draw an arrow to show the incoming direction and the outgoing direction of the marble on the paper underneath the mystery shape. You may want to use letters or numbers to keep track of which rolls go together. Repeat multiple times from different locations and angles. Mark each trial on the same piece of paper. If the object is small, you will have multiple straight lines and that is OK. It helps you determine the size of the unknown shape.

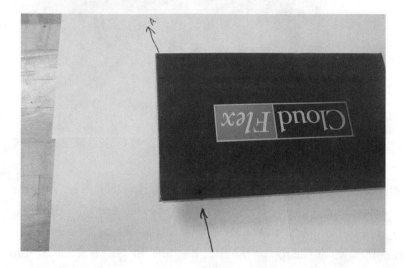

Step 5: Slowly slide the piece of paper out without looking under the shoe box lid.

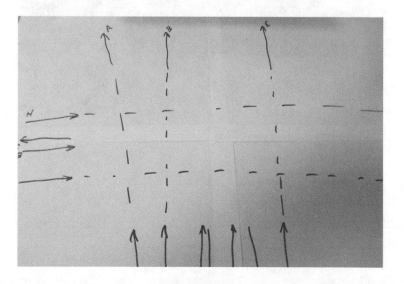

Step 6: It will be easier if you connect the traces that went straight through under the shoe box lid. This will allow you to know the overall size. From the traces on your paper, draw what you think the hidden object looks like.

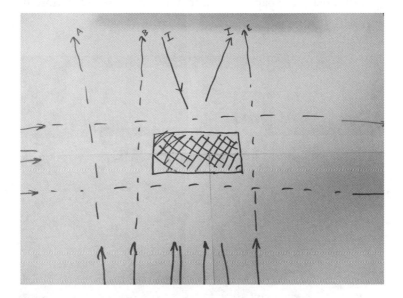

Step 7: Remove the shoe box lid and check your model against the actual shape. You will get better with practice.

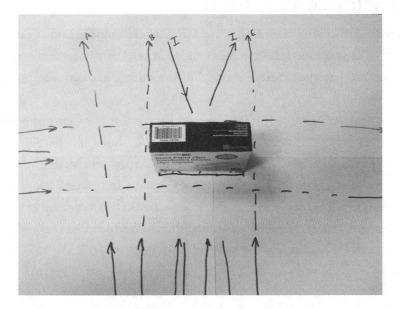

Step 8: Repeat with a partner for other shapes. Take turns being the hider and the scientist. Once you are fairly good at determining individual shapes, try putting several shapes together to create funky shapes. (For teachers, you can set up multiple shapes at different lab stations and have each group replace the paper before they rotate to a new station. But most students will want to peek.)

The Science Behind It

More than almost any science, chemistry uses models of things that can't be seen. You will never see inside an atom, only a model of what scientists think it looks like. You have just created a model of something you can't see, just like a chemist would.

New Zealand's Ernest Rutherford used almost the exact same process to create his model of the atom in the early 1900s. He shot alpha particles—large positive pieces—at a very thin piece of gold foil. Most went straight through. Some were bent a little bit. But some turned around and came back. Since like charges repel, he deduced that the atoms of gold had very tiny, extremely strong centers. His early model was called the Rutherford Planetary Model. Today we call this extremely tiny positive center the nucleus. We have adapted the model over the years as our science technology has gotten better.

Candy Atoms

Make atom models from junk drawer items, or make them good enough to eat. Edible Candy Atoms are more tasty.

From the Junk Drawer:

□ 3 different objects, like pushpins, paper clips, and safety pins, or three different coins

□ For an edible atom, use 3 different types of candy, like Butterscotches, Peppermints, and Root Beer Barrels

□ 2 pieces of paper

□ Pen

Step 1: Separate your items into three piles. One pile represents protons, which are positive and reside in the center of the nucleus. Another pile represents neutrons, which are neutral and also reside in the center of the nucleus. The last pile represents electrons, which are negative and orbit around the nucleus. On one piece of paper, write down which objects represent which parts. Shown are several options for your atom parts. You just need three different types of subatomic particles. For candy, color is a great way to separate the three parts of the atom. (In class, I usually use colored candies like Skittles, M&M'S, or Gummy Bears, but they don't photograph well in black and white.)

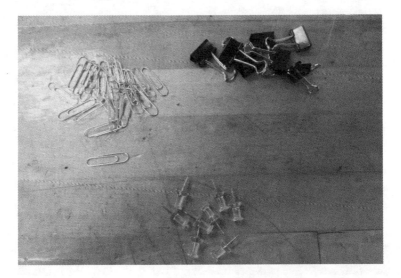

Step 2: Draw a small circle at the center of a sheet of paper. This circle will represent the nucleus of an atom. Draw two larger circles around the nucleus as shown.

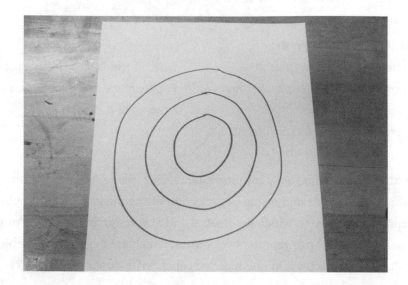

Step 3: Place one proton in the center circle. Place one electron on the innermost of the larger circles. You have just created a model of the hydrogen atom. Hydrogen is the most plentiful element in the universe. The simplest form of hydrogen does not have any neutrons.

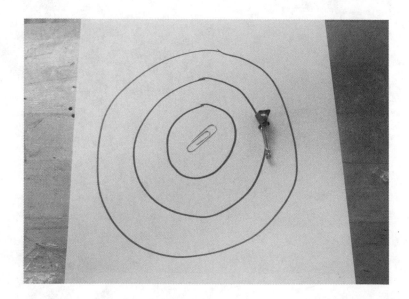

Step 4: Add a neutron to the nucleus of your hydrogen atom. You have created another form of hydrogen. Hydrogen always has just one proton. By varying the number of neutrons, however, you can create isotopes of hydrogen.

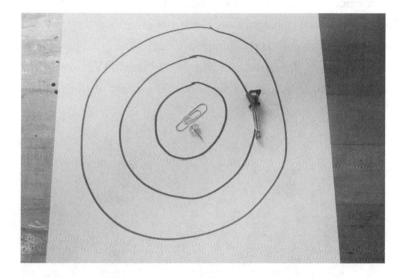

Step 5: Now for another atom. Place two protons and two neutrons in the center of the sheet. Place two electrons on the first (innermost) large circle. You have just created a model of helium. You could add more neutrons, but having two protons always means you have a helium atom.

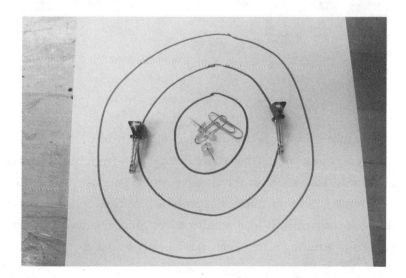

Step 6: You can continue and make all of the atoms that exist in nature. You would have to have a lot of candy, since the largest natural atom has 92 protons, 92 electrons, and more than 100 neutrons! Perhaps you should build a smaller one. Place seven protons and seven neutrons in the center. (You may need to stack them up.) Place seven electrons on the outside, following one more rule: only two electrons can go on the innermost large circle. Put the next five on the outermost circle. You have just created a model of nitrogen, the most abundant gas in the air. We breathe nitrogen in and out all the time, as it makes up about 80 percent of the air around us.

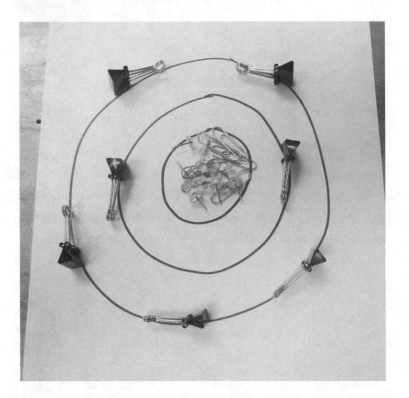

Step 7: Now take a look at how atoms become electrically charged. All atoms start neutral, which means they start with the same number of protons and electrons. Take a look at the nitrogen model you just created. Remove two electrons. Count the number of protons (positive) and the number of electrons (negative). Which number wins? Since you have two extra positives, the resulting nitrogen ion has a positive-two charge.

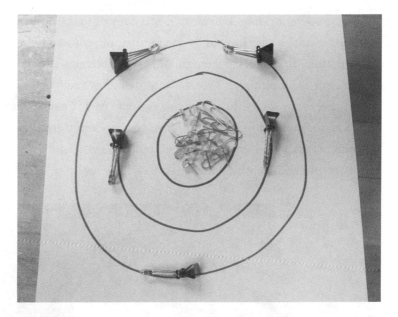

Step 8: Now add back the two electrons to re-create your original nitrogen model. Now add one extra electron. Count the number of protons (positive) and the number of electrons (negative) again. Which number wins? Since you now have one extra electron (negative), the resulting nitrogen ion has a negative-one charge.

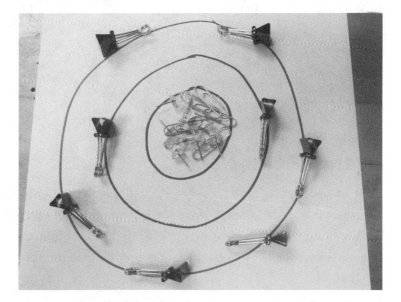

Step 9: Use a computer or science book to find a copy of the periodic table and build a larger atom. You are limited by the number of protons you have. And remember that the first level can contain only two electrons. The second level can contain only eight electrons. Don't worry about how many electrons to put in the other outer circles. Just add whatever you decide to the next level. You will learn more about that in future science classes. The atom pictured below is number 12. Use the periodic table to find element number 12. That element is contained in anything that is alive or has ever lived.

The Science Behind It

You have just learned how to build the Rutherford-Bohr Planetary Model. Rutherford came up with the concept of the nucleus, and Danish scientist Niels Bohr discovered that electrons orbit at different distances from the nucleus. Scientists have further revised the model over the years and are still revising it today.

The periodic table is like a roster for a sports game. It tells you what each element is based on the number of protons. Atoms of the same element always have the same number of protons. For example, all oxygen atoms contain eight protons. Nine protons and you have a different element. The number of neutrons can vary slightly. Oxygen normally has eight neutrons, but is sometimes found in nature with seven neutrons and sometimes with ten neutrons. But as long as there are eight protons, you have oxygen.

Losing or gaining electrons is common and creates an *ion*. An ion is simply an electrically charged atom. If an atom gains electrons, the ion created becomes negative, since the electrons are negative. If an atom loses electrons, it will create a positive ion, since it will have extra protons.

Positive and negative ions will join together to form compounds. Remember that unlike charges attract, so positive ions stick to negative ions. Table salt is a great example of this. Sodium atoms lose an electron and become positive. The chlorine atom gains the electron that sodium lost and becomes negative. The sodium ion and the chlorine ion then join together and create a really strong chemical bond.

All atoms start neutral, but luckily they don't stay that way. Trading and sharing electrons allows all sorts of compounds to be formed. All candies probably contain only ten or fewer elements, but they can combine in a multitude of tasty ways.

Junk Drawer Periodic Table

Organize your junk drawer and learn about the periodic table.

From the Junk Drawer:

☐ Everything

☐ Copy of the periodic table (from a book or online)

Step 1: Take a look at the contents of your junk drawer. It could be a family junk drawer or maybe the junk drawer in your bedroom. Some people use a sock drawer (or a drawer in a jewelry box) in their bedroom as a junk drawer.

Step 2: Take the contents out, look at the stuff you have, and decide how to separate it. Put things that go together in piles. Be creative, but understand why you put things together.

Step 3: For a normal family junk drawer, you may end up with several common piles. One pile could be writing tools, which would include pens, pencils, crayons, and so forth. Another pile might be things to hold stuff together, which could include tape, glue, thumbtacks, brads, and paper clips. You might also have a pile of tools, like scissors and screwdrivers, and a pile of paper stuff, like coupons and letters. Maybe you have a pile of coins, buttons, and other miscellaneous stuff. A bedroom junk drawer might have a pile of toys and a pile of other things. Take one pile and line the objects up in a column with the smallest at the top and the largest at the bottom. Repeat for the next pile, putting the column next to the column made from the first pile. You have created your own Junk Drawer Periodic Table.

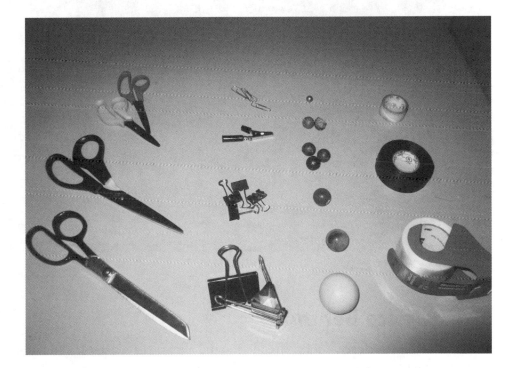

Step 4: Now look at an actual periodic table from a book or online. The vertical columns are called families. Families have similar properties, just like your columns have similar properties. The bigger elements are near the bottom, just like in your Junk Drawer Periodic Table. When you are done, clean up and put stuff back into the junk drawer with some order. Your parents will be happy and you have learned something. You can repurpose some old disposable plastic or Styrofoam cups to help you out. After they are cleaned, use scissors to cut the cups down so the drawer will close.

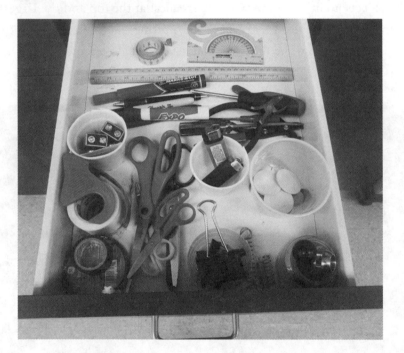

The Science Behind It

A Russian science teacher, Dmitri Mendeleev, did almost the exact same thing in the 1860s. He took the 56 known elements and wrote down what was known about each element on index cards. He grouped his cards by similar properties and then created columns. Out of his research grew our modern day periodic table. He even predicted the properties of elements that weren't discovered until later. Today there are more than 110 known elements, and scientists still use Mendeleev's structure for the table.

J is the only letter that doesn't show up on the periodic table.

Breaking Water

Split water into parts using a 9-volt battery.

Adult supervision required

From the Junk Drawer:

- Rinsed, empty clear plastic drink bottle or clear plastic cup
- Scissors
- 9-volt battery
- Marker
- 2 metal thumbtacks
- Water
- Baking soda

Step 1: If you are using a drink bottle, get adult help to cut the bottle in half. If you are using a clear plastic cup, you can just use scissors to cut down the side and then around the cup to make it shorter. Hold a 9-volt battery near the bottom of the cup and mark where the two battery terminals are with a marker, as shown.

Step 2: Press a metal thumbtack through the bottom of the cup at each mark. If you do not wiggle the thumbtacks, they should be watertight. But you may want to do this experiment over a kitchen counter just to be safe.

Step 3: Add about an inch of water to the plastic cup. Add a small spoonful of baking soda to the water. Swirl the cup to get the baking soda to dissolve.

Step 4: Stand the 9-volt battery up on the kitchen counter. Lower the plastic cup of water until both battery terminals touch the heads of the thumbtacks.

Step 5: Observe the points of the thumbtacks inside the water. What do you see? Look carefully and you will see that one tack will be bubbling faster than the other.

The Science Behind It

You probably already know that the formula for water is H_2O. You probably also know that hydrogen and oxygen are gases. The experiment you just did was to separate water into oxygen and hydrogen gas. This process is called *electrolysis*. Anytime you use electricity to separate parts of a compound, the process is called electrolysis.

The baking soda served as an electrolyte to help the water conduct electricity. Pure water doesn't actually conduct electricity. But pure water is very hard to find since water dissolves so many things. As a matter of fact, water is called the universal solvent because it is so good at dissolving stuff.

If you looked closely, you saw more gas coming from one thumbtack point than the other. Look at the formula for water and you can figure out which gas is more plentiful in water. The reason electrolysis works is because a battery has a positive terminal and a negative terminal. Water also has a positive part (hydrogen) and a negative part (oxygen). It's amazing that water is a liquid even though it is actually composed of two gases. Compounds like water often have very different properties than the elements (hydrogen and oxygen) that make them up.

Joseph Priestley is credited with "discovering" oxygen. He developed a chemical reaction that would yield pure oxygen. Oxygen is around us, as you know, but it makes up less than 20 percent of what we breathe. Priestley also invented soda water (carbonated water). Pharmacists in the United States started adding syrup to the soda water to create soft drinks like Coke and Pepsi.

Tape Repulsion

Learn the secrets of electrons with ordinary tape.

From the Junk Drawer:

☐ Clear plastic tape

Step 1: Tear off a piece of clear plastic tape approximately 12 inches long. Fold 1 inch over at the end to create a non-sticky handle. Press the sticky part down to a smooth surface such as a countertop, making sure to hang the handle you made off the edge of the countertop. Use your fingers to press down hard along the entire length of the sticky part. Note: To make it easier to photograph, fancy patterned tape was used. Clear tape works just as well and is cheaper.

Step 2: Repeat step 1 with another 12-inch strip of tape.

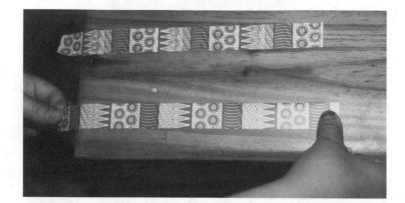

Step 3: One at a time, pull each piece of tape off the countertop, using the handles. Hold only the handles, trying not to touch the sticky part of the tape. With one strip in each hand, position the non-sticky sides of the dangling pieces so that they face each other. Now slowly move the tape pieces toward one another and observe what happens. Why do you think they repel (push away from) each other?

Step 4: Press a new piece of tape down on the counter again as in step 1. Make sure to leave the handle hanging over the edge of the countertop. Now create another strip with a handle. Place the sticky part of this tape directly on top of the first piece. Press firmly down the entire sticky length.

Step 5: Remove the top piece of tape by pulling on the handle. Remove the bottom piece with your other hand. Slowly bring the two pieces close together and observe what happens. Why do you think they now attract?

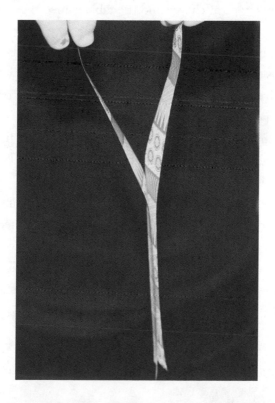

The Science Behind It

The science here is a result of the electric charges that make up atoms. Atoms have three parts. Protons are positive and exist in the center of the atom, the nucleus. Neutrons are neutral and act like glue to keep the nucleus together. Electrons are negative and orbit around the nucleus. The simplest way to think of an atom is in terms of the solar system. The nucleus is like the sun and the electrons are like planets. (In reality, it is more complicated, as you will learn later.)

There are several rules governing electric charges. First, all atoms start out neutral, but can lose or gain electrons. Only electrons can move, since they are on the outside of the atom. Second, like charges (such as two positives) repel and unlike charges (positive and negative) attract.

In steps 1 through 3, the strips of tape repelled each other. The strips had the exact same electrical charge. You can't tell whether it is positive or negative, but since they repel, you can deduce that they are the same. When you pressed the tape down, you caused a charge to move from the countertop to the tape. The tape gained one type of charge and the table gained the other type.

It would be easy to say that electrons were the only thing transferred, but scientists think it might be more complicated than that. Studies have shown that entire groups of molecules can be pulled away, bringing with them extra negative or positive charges. Either way, the tape pieces repel one another. They have the same charge.

In steps 4 through 6, the tape pieces attracted. Therefore they have opposite charges. One tape strip gained a charge from the other. One strip is positive and one strip is negative.

Atoms can become electrically charged by losing or gaining electrons. Charged atoms are called ions. And positive ions like to connect to negative ions. Positive ions and negative ions can form compounds because they are electrically attracted. Table salt is composed of a positive sodium ion and a negative chlorine ion. They stick together and form the crystals that you sprinkle on food.

Rainbow Ice

Make beautiful ice and learn a secret about water.

From the Junk Drawer:

- [ ] A few empty balloons
- [ ] Water
- [ ] Food coloring
- [ ] Fabric tape measure (optional)
- [ ] Plastic bowl
- [ ] Freezer
- [ ] Scissors
- [ ] Ice tray (optional)

Step 1: New balloons come with a powder inside to keep them from sticking to themselves. Use water to rinse out the balloons before you start. Then put a few drops of food coloring inside an empty balloon.

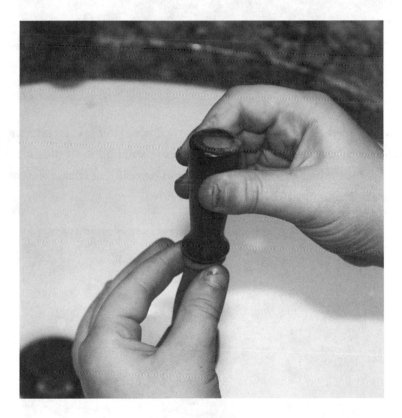

Step 2: Stretch the balloon over the end of the faucet, turn the water on lightly, and partially fill the balloon with water. If you want to use the rainbow ice in a drink, you will want the rainbow ice balls to be small enough to fit in a glass. But you can make them any size you want. For an option, wrap a fabric tape measure around the biggest part of the balloon to measure the circumference and write down the measurement.

Step 3: When the balloon is big enough, turn the water off. To take the balloon off, pinch the top very tightly before you pull it off the faucet. Tie a knot in the balloon. Make more and experiment with different colors and combinations of colors in each balloon.

Step 4: Place the filled balloons inside the freezer in a plastic bowl for at least two hours.

Step 5: Take the balloons out of the freezer. If you measured the balloons' circumferences with a tape measure before they froze, do it again. The balloons have grown because the ice expanded. Use scissors to cut the knots off the balloons. Each balloon will also usually have a small air pocket, so you can put the point of the scissors into the air pocket to cut the balloon. Use your fingers to peel the rest of the balloon off and throw away the scraps. There is usually some food coloring left on the inside of the balloon, so do this over a sink or bowl. Rinsing the Rainbow Ice in water will remove the extra food coloring. It might stain your fingers a bit, but it will wash off with a little scrubbing.

Step 6: Place a few rainbow ice balls in a clear glass or bowl to admire them. Rainbow ice balls are perfect for parties. You can also skip the balloons and just add food coloring to each individual compartment of an old-fashioned ice tray.

The Science Behind It

Water is a unique substance. Most substances get smaller as they cool down. But as water freezes, it actually gets bigger. That is the reason that a glass bottle full of water will break if put in the freezer. The water expands as it freezes and breaks the glass. Water freezing is very powerful and will even cause car engine blocks to crack in really cold environments if you don't use antifreeze. In super cold environments (like northern Alaska), they make motors with a built-in electric heater that needs to be plugged in while the car or truck is parked in cold weather.

In this experiment you also get to play with food coloring. Food coloring is a safe type of dye. The colors mix in the same way as pigments in art class. Experiment to create your favorite color. And share your rainbow ice with friends. Make sure you use new balloons from a package if you are going to drink from the glass.

Three-fourths of all of the fresh water in the world is contained in frozen glaciers.

Balloon Secret

Learn why a balloon is so hard to blow up the first time.

From the Junk Drawer:

☐ Rubber band
☐ 2 balloons
☐ Empty cereal box, file folder, or construction paper

☐ Ruler
☐ Scissors
☐ Tape
☐ 50–100 paper clips

Step 1: Stretch a rubber band and let it go. What happened? The rubber band snaps back because rubber is elastic. Elastic compounds will stretch, but they like to go back to their original shape.

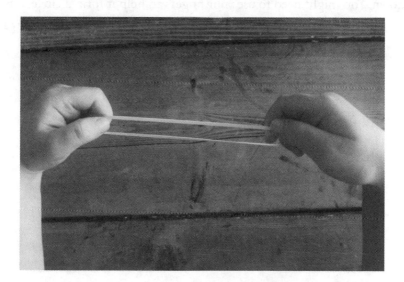

Step 2: Find two identically sized new balloons. Stretch one balloon with your hands four or five times. (More on why you do that later.) Blow up the balloon you just stretched. Let the air out. What did you observe as you blew up the balloon? When was the balloon hardest to blow up? Blow the same balloon up several times and let it deflate each time. Now lay the new balloon on the tabletop next to the deflated one you blew up several times. What do you notice about the two balloons? Why do you think that happened?

Step 3: Find an empty cereal box, file folder, or construction paper. Cut a 1-inch-by-6-inch strip. Tape the strip end to end so it forms a circle, as shown. You might need to use your fingers to help it form a circle. Lay it down on the tabletop so that it looks like a circle when you look down at it.

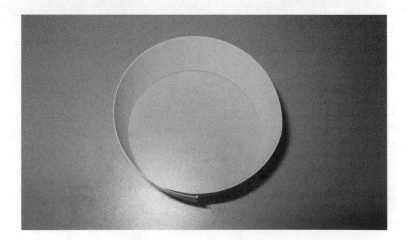

Step 4: Now cut a 1-inch-by-10-inch strip and tape the ends together. Lay this circle around the smaller circle from the last step. Dump 50 to 100 paper clips between the two circles. The number is not important, just make sure you use the same quantity for step 5 and step 7. Use your fingers to spread the paper clips evenly around the inside circle. Instead of paper clips, you can use candies like M&M'S or Skittles. Marbles or BBs also work great and you don't have to use your fingers, because they roll. (Note to teachers: I use BBs when I do this in class, but not every kid has BBs anymore.) The paper clips represent rubber molecules and the two circles represent the inner and outer surface of the balloon. Look at how many paper clips are touching other paper clips—they are stacked on top of each other. Each paper clip would tug on several other paper clips if they were rubber molecules.

Step 5: Now cut another strip, 1 inch by 14 inches. Use tape to secure the ends and stand it up just like in the previous two steps. Take the larger circle from step 4—this will represent the *inside* of the balloon—and place it inside the new, larger ring. Take all of the paper clips (or candies, marbles, etc.) from the small "balloon" circle in step 5 and put them in the larger "balloon" circle. Use your fingers to spread them out again. The paper clips still represent the number of rubber molecules in the balloon. Look at how many paper clips are touching other paper clips now. Make a new hypothesis. Why is there less "tug" as the balloon increases in size?

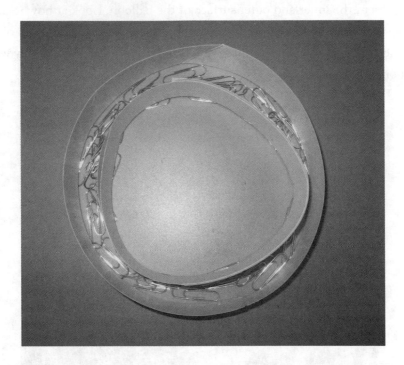

The Science Behind It

All elastic compounds can be stretched. And after they are stretched, their molecules tug each other and they try to go back to their original shape. Rubber balloons and rubber bands do this, but so does the elastic in your socks and underwear.

When you first pick up a new balloon, the rubber molecules are very close together. That means they are touching thousands of other rubber molecules. Remember, molecules are incredibly tiny. When you stretch the balloon with your hands, you are stretching the rubber molecules a little. Some rubber molecules will stay stretched out a tiny bit. Stretching the balloon lessens the force required from your lungs a tiny bit. When you looked at the balloons in step 2, the stretched one was larger. The larger one is easier to blow up. Always stretch your balloons a few times before you blow them up.

Any balloon has a fixed number of molecules, and that number is way more than the number of "rubber molecules" you used—a greater number of rubber molecules than you could ever count. When you first blow up a balloon, even if you stretched it, the molecules are very tightly packed. Your lungs have to work extra hard to get the balloon started. And after the balloon starts to inflate, the number of molecules is still the same. But since the walls of the balloon get thinner, each rubber molecule has fewer other molecules to tug on. It is easier to blow up the balloon as it gets bigger. There is still a limit to how big the balloon can get. Keep blowing and the rubber molecules will tear away from each other and you will hear a loud pop.

Latex balloons come from rubber trees. The rubber tree's bark is cut and the latex is caught in a cup. Harvesting the latex doesn't hurt the tree. A rubber tree can produce latex for 40 years.

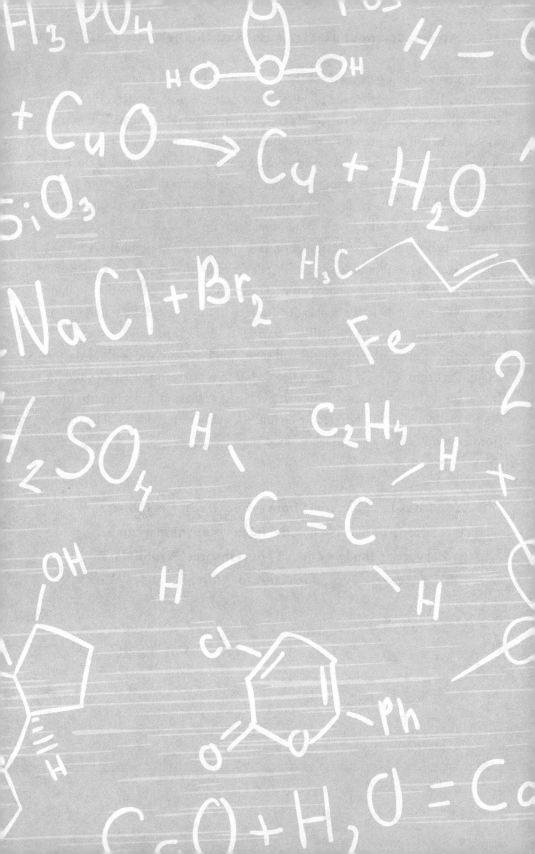

3

Solutions

Solutions are liquids that have other elements or compounds dissolved in them. From iced tea to milk to shampoo, solutions are all around us. Solutions have different densities and different properties, and they allow us to exist. Sometimes they combine, like mixing two flavors of soda at a soda fountain. But other times they don't mix easily, like oil and vinegar in Italian dressing. Solutions can also make solids behave in strange ways.

Pop in a Glass

Float a popcorn kernel between two layers.

From the Junk Drawer:

☐ Honey
☐ Clear glass jar or plastic bottle
☐ Popcorn kernels
☐ Water

Step 1: Pour about 1 inch of honey in a glass jar. You could also use a plastic bottle with the label removed.

Step 2: Drop five or six kernels of raw, uncooked popcorn into the honey. The kernels will float on top.

Step 3: Slowly add water by tilting the glass and letting a stream of water slide down the inside of the glass above the honey.

Step 4: Stand the glass up and let the honey settle. What do you observe?

The Science Behind It

Solutions don't always mix together, but in this case they can if you are not careful. The honey in this experiment has the greatest density, so it sinks to the bottom. The popcorn kernels have some water inside—that is what makes the kernel pop when heated—but the rest of the popcorn gives it a density greater than water. However, the kernels' density is less than the honey. The kernels float in the middle of the solution. (Honey will dissolve in water if shaken or stirred; that is why you added the water very slowly.)

This same process is used for fluid-filled paperweights and magnets sold at many aquariums and science museums, but the manufacturers use liquids that will never dissolve in each other. The paperweights have a dolphin or a whale that always floats between two liquids. Objects in liquids float because of density. Ice floats in water because it has less density than water.

Mysterious Floating Egg

Float an egg in the middle of a glass of water.

From the Junk Drawer:

☐ Clear cup or glass
☐ Water
☐ Salt
☐ Spoon
☐ Raw egg

Step 1: Fill a cup about ⅓ full with water. Stir in a giant spoonful of salt. You can also use leftover fast food packets of salt, but you will need at least six.

Step 2: Gently place the egg in the cup of salt water.

Step 3: Slowly pour regular water in on top of the egg. It is usually best to keep the stream of pouring water hitting the top of the egg as you pour. Fill up the cup and observe what happens.

Step 4: Put your head down at eye level with the cup and observe. What do you see? Why do you think that happened?

The Science Behind It

Objects float because of density, as you learned earlier. When you add salt to water, the salt actually "hides" inside the water. The saltwater is more dense because the mass is now much greater, but the volume is only a tiny bit larger. In the same way, you can float more easily in the saltwater ocean than in a freshwater swimming pool.

Since a raw egg is slightly more dense than regular water, it sinks below the regular water. But the raw egg's density is less than the saltwater. Therefore the egg floats in the middle of the cup.

Fresh eggs sink and stale eggs float in regular water.
Air actually passes right through the eggshell, just very slowly.
An egg that completely floats in water should be discarded.

Sweet Crystals

Make your own candy.

Adult supervision required

From the Junk Drawer:

☐ Craft sticks
☐ Pencils
☐ Rubber bands
☐ 2 glass jars
☐ Water
☐ Saucepan
☐ Measuring cup
☐ Sugar
☐ Spoon
☐ Flavored extract (optional)
☐ Paper towels
☐ Fork
☐ Small kitchen strainer

Step 1: Prepare a craft stick for the Sweet Crystals. Use a rubber band to attach the craft stick to the middle of a pencil as shown. You will probably have enough liquid for at least two Sweet Crystal sticks, so prepare at least two craft sticks. You can also use pipe cleaners or bamboo skewers instead of the sticks.

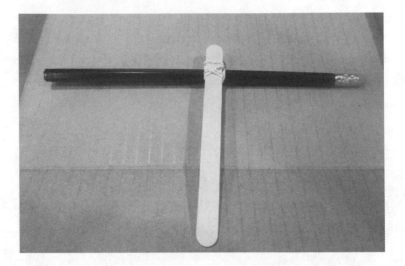

Step 2: Lay the pencil across the top of an empty jar. Adjust the stick so that it doesn't touch the sides or the bottom of the jar. You want to have a 1-inch clearance from the bottom.

Step 3: **You will now need adult help** to create the supersaturated solution that is the basis for this experiment. Add 1 cup of water to a saucepan on the stove.

Step 4: Add 3 cups of sugar and a few drops of food coloring to the water. Heat over medium heat while stirring with a spoon. For a flavored Sweet Crystal stick, you can add a few drops of a flavored extract from the spice cabinet in your kitchen. Be careful and don't add much, as extracts are very strong.

Step 5: Keep a close eye on the saucepan and continue stirring the solution. As soon as it starts to boil, remove it from the heat. The liquid should be milky to almost clear.

Step 6: Take the stick out of the glass. With adult help, carefully pour the sugar solution into the glass. Pour it almost all the way to the top.

Step 7: Dip the bottom 3 inches of the craft stick in the sugar solution. Put some sugar in a cup and push the wet part of the stick into the sugar. Turn it over to make sure both sides are covered. You may need to use your fingers to make sure all of the wet part of the stick is covered with sugar. The sugar crystals that stick will give the Sweet Crystals a place to start growing.

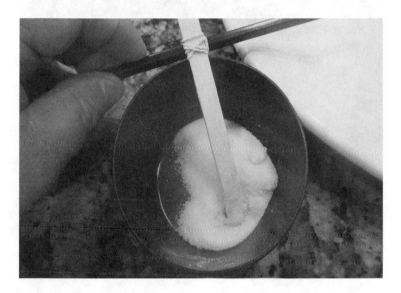

Step 8: Slide the craft stick back into the glass. Make sure the stick is not touching the sides or bottom.

Step 9: Put the Sweet Crystals glass in a safe, out-of-the-way place in the kitchen. Cover the top with a paper towel to keep dust out. Tear a small hole in the paper towel to help keep the stick upright. It will take several days to grow your Sweet Crystals.

Step 10: The next day, pull out the stick and observe. What do you see?

Step 11: On the second day, you want to move your solution to a clean jar. Remove the stick and set it off to the side. You may need a fork to break the crystal "skin" on the surface of the sugar solution. Use the fork to remove and discard as many crystals as possible.

Step 12: Pour the liquid into a clean jar. If you have a small kitchen strainer, use it to help catch any loose crystals as you pour the liquid into the new jar. Hang the stick back in the sugar solution to grow more crystals. Look at the first jar. Notice how crystals have grown on the sides and bottom. If you don't switch to a clean jar, the entire jar will crystallize. The same process will happen in your refrigerator with jelly if it is left too long.

Step 13: On day three, pull the stick out and observe. How is the Sweet Crystals stick different from the day before? You can repeat step 12 and clean the jar again, but every second day is usually often enough. On the fifth day, you can take it out to drip dry if you are impatient. Just place it on a plate for an hour to dry before you start nibbling. You can also wait two more days and repeat step 12 again if you choose. Be careful that the stick doesn't crystallize to the jar sides. Enjoy and remember to brush your teeth well when you finish eating your Sweet Crystals.

The Science Behind It

What you have created is called rock candy. By adding a large amount of sugar to the water, you are creating a saturated solution of sugar (and any flavoring or color you added). By doing it on the stovetop you can add more sugar because heat allows all solutions to dissolve more solute. *Solute* is the fancy name for a solid that you put inside a solution, like sugar in sweet tea. You have a solution that is packed with dissolved sugar.

As the water evaporates over the next few days, the sugar crystals will form on the stick. The shapes they form represent the shape of sugar crystals. The large crystals could be smashed into tiny crystals like those you buy from the grocery store. But the large crystals are neater to look at. And they taste good too.

Lemons have more sugar than strawberries if you have the
exact same amount of each.

Milk Art

Turn milk into a work of art.

From the Junk Drawer:

☐ Plate   ☐ Q-tip
☐ Milk (non-skim works well)   ☐ Dish soap
☐ Food coloring

Step 1: Pour milk into a plate until the bottom is covered. Add a few drops of
food coloring at different places in the milk.

Step 2: Put some dish soap on one end of a Q-tip. Place the soapy end of the Q-tip into the center of one of the food color drops. You can have multiple people working on art at the same time.

Step 3: Repeat for the other drops. You can make more plates and experiment with mixing colors. You might even want to take pictures of all your artwork. Clean up when you are finished.

The Science Behind It

The secret behind this experiment is the soap. The food coloring just floats on the milk until soap is added to the mix. Adding soap lowers the surface tension, which allows the food coloring to more easily flow around the surface of the milk. The soap also breaks the fat molecules in the milk apart. As the fat molecules break, the food coloring goes with them, and since the surface tension is lower, they float around. Breaking down fat and grease molecules is what allows soap to clean stuff.

> **Dynamite can be made from peanuts—stay away if you are allergic! Peanuts can be processed to create glycerin, one of the ingredients in dynamite. You can also create glycerin from almost any type of natural oil or animal fat.**

Not-So-Permanent Marker

Watch the colors run!

Adult supervision required

From the Junk Drawer:

☐ Paper towel or coffee filter
☐ Scissors
☐ Cup
☐ Black permanent marker
☐ Rubbing alcohol (any strength)

Step 1: Cut a 1-inch strip of paper towel (or coffee filter).

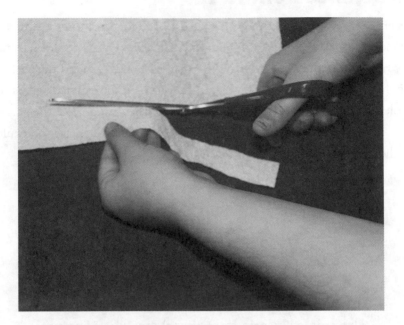

Step 2: Fold the strip so it hangs over the edge of the cup. You want the inside piece of the paper towel strip to stop just short of the bottom of the cup, as shown.

Step 3: Use a permanent marker to make a thick black mark about 1 inch from the bottom of the strip.

Step 4: Pour about ¾ inch of rubbing alcohol into the cup. It is important that the alcohol be below the marker line when you place the paper towel strip back over the edge of the cup.

Step 5: Hang the paper strip over the edge of the cup. Make sure the bottom of the paper strip dips into the alcohol, but the marker line is *not* in the alcohol.

Step 6: Observe what happens over the next 30 minutes. What do you see? Leave it undisturbed and look at it the next day. Pull the strip out and unfold it. Have the colors spread even more? You can repeat the experiment with different color permanent markers.

The Science Behind It

All ink is composed of pigments. A pigment is a molecule that absorbs particular colors of light and reflects the colors of light that we see. As you probably learned in art class, the three primary color pigments are yellow, cyan (a shade of blue), and magenta (a shade of red). These are also the three color cartridges needed for a color printer. Every color can be made from these three pigment colors.

Black is a combination of pigment colors. Alcohol wicks up the paper towel into the black marker line you drew. The pigment molecules will then be carried up the paper towel. The lighter, smaller, and more soluble molecules travel farthest up the paper strip. You get to see what pigment colors make up your black marker (or whatever color you used). This process is called chromatography.

Although oxygen gas is colorless, both the liquid and solid form are blue.

Chalk Chromatography

Add a little extra color to your sidewalk chalk.

From the Junk Drawer:

☐ Water
☐ Plastic cup
☐ Sidewalk chalk (or regular chalk)
☐ Washable marker

Step 1: Pour about ¾ inch of water into a cup.

Step 2: Using a washable marker, draw a line around the piece of chalk about 1 inch from one end. (Note for teachers: Vis-a-Vis markers also work well.)

Step 3: Stand the chalk up in the water. Make sure the marker line is above the water to start.

Step 4: Watch over the next five minutes as the water wicks up the chalk. What do you observe? Leave it longer and go back and look later in the day or the next morning.

Optional Step 5: You can also repeat the experiment using normal skinny chalk and a bottle cap. Fill the bottle cap half full of water.

Optional Step 6: Draw a line around the skinny chalk with a washable marker.

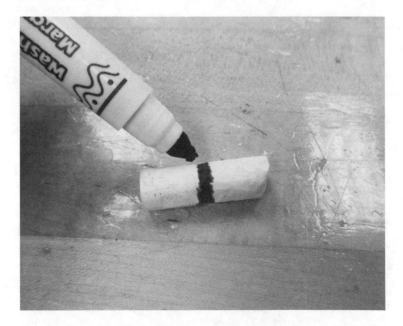

Optional Step 7: Stand the chalk up in the bottle cap.

Optional Step 8: Watch over the next five minutes as the water wicks up the chalk. What do you observe? Leave it longer and go back and look later in the day or the next morning.

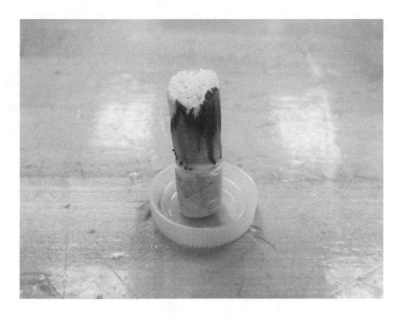

The Science Behind It

The ink used in washable markers dissolves in water, which is why they are washable. Water dissolves the ink and your clothes come clean. In this experiment, you used water to separate the pigments in the water soluble ink. (For a permanent marker, as in the previous experiment, you need alcohol to separate the pigment colors.) The water wicks up the chalk. As the water rises up the chalk, it separates the pigments by their size and their solubility. The smaller, more soluble pigments rise up the chalk the farthest. The chalk absorbs the water and allows it to rise up. The color will only penetrate the outside layers of the chalk. Your chalk will still show mostly the inside color when you write with it. But the chalk looks neater in the box.

Energy Drink Tester

Create a tester for electrolytes.

From the Junk Drawer:

☐ Small LED flashlight

☐ 2 batteries, AA or AAA

☐ Electrical tape

☐ Scissors

☐ Aluminum foil or copper wire

☐ Cup or glass

☐ Water

☐ Salt

☐ Spoon

☐ Energy drink (optional)

Step 1: Unscrew the top of a small LED flashlight. Look carefully at the flashlight head. All flashlight bulb assemblies will have two metal pieces. One is at the end of the bulb assembly opposite the bulb. The other metal piece will be on the side behind the bulb. The batteries and the housing for the batteries will connect those two metal points to make the complete circuit to light the bulb. You will not be using the housing for this project, just the batteries and the head assembly.

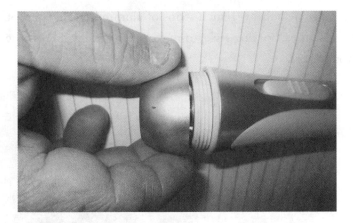

Step 2: Push the two batteries together, facing the same direction, and use a strip of electrical tape to hold them together. A helpful hint: use scissors to cut a piece of tape about 4 inches long before you attempt to tape the batteries together.

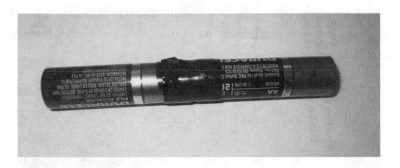

Step 3: Hold the head assembly and the batteries together and use another 4-inch strip of electrical tape to keep them together. The head assembly and the batteries should be tight and stay together. Retape if they aren't tight.

Step 4: Cut two 4-inch-by-1-inch strips of aluminum foil. Fold each of the pieces four times, hot dog style, to make them stronger. Press the strips flat with your finger.

Step 5: Attach one end of the first strip to the metal side of the flashlight assembly using electrical tape. The aluminum strip should be tight, but hang freely so that it can be bent to fit into your cup. You can use copper wire instead of the aluminum foil if you have any.

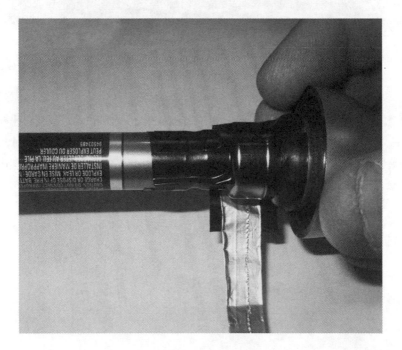

Step 6: Attach the other strip to the end of the batteries securely with electrical tape. Use the piece of tape across the end of the battery and pull it tight. You can test your connection by touching the two aluminum strips together. The light should come on if your connections are tight. Repair any connections if the light doesn't come on.

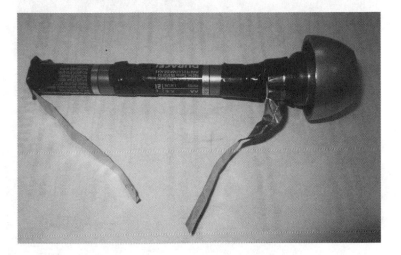

Step 7: Fill a cup about three-fourths full with water. Add at least two big spoonfuls of salt to your cup of water and stir.

Step 8: Turn the lights off in the room. Lower both aluminum strips into the salt water. What do you observe? Add two more spoonfuls of salt and try it again. Is it different now? You can use the same device to test an energy drink (like Gatorade) if you have one.

The Science Behind It

Electrolytes are liquids that contain a substance that will split into a positive part and a negative part in water. Chemists call this *ionizing* a compound. Electricity is the flow of negative electrons. Since the compound is ionized it can conduct electricity.

Electrolytes are necessary for your body. Your brain tells your muscles to perform tasks by sending an electric impulse down your nerves to the appropriate muscles. Electrolytes are needed in your nerves to conduct this electricity. As you sweat, you lose electrolytes. That is why sweat tastes salty. Sweat is actually saltwater. When exercising, you need to replace the electrolytes you sweat out. When you aren't exercising, energy drinks are just empty calories.

The electrolyte conducts electricity and lights up the bulb in this tester. The number of ions in the solution determines how bright the light gets. A few ions and the light will hardly be visible. The more ions there are, the brighter the light. You could keep adding table salt to see how bright the bulb gets.

Gatorade was invented by researchers at the University of
Florida working in conjunction with the athletic teams. It is
the biggest selling electrolyte drink in the world. University of
Florida's mascot is the Gator.

My Soda Has Gas

Capture the gas from a bottle of soda and you'll be amazed how much you get.

Adult supervision required

From the Junk Drawer:

☐ Outside area

☐ Balloon

☐ Salt or sugar

☐ Full bottle of carbonated soda
(any type)

Step 1: Find a suitable place to do this outside in case the balloon comes off
or breaks. Pour one heaping tablespoon of salt into the balloon. You can
also use sugar, and you don't have to measure the amount exactly. Put the
balloon off to the side.

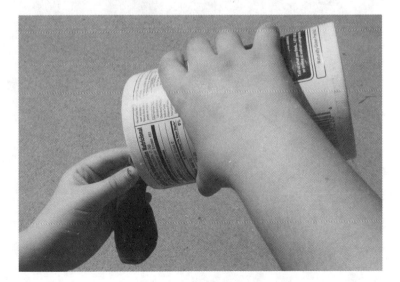

Step 2: Hold a bottle of soda with one hand and gently remove the top. You want to capture all the gas, so avoid moving the bottle as much as possible.

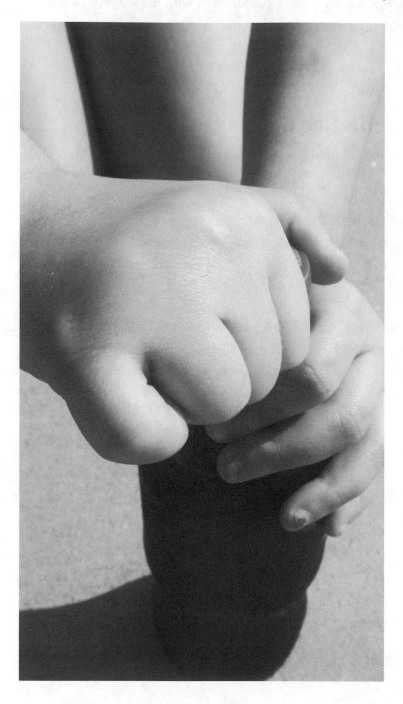

Step 3: While letting the balloon hang down to the side, stretch the neck over the top of the bottle.

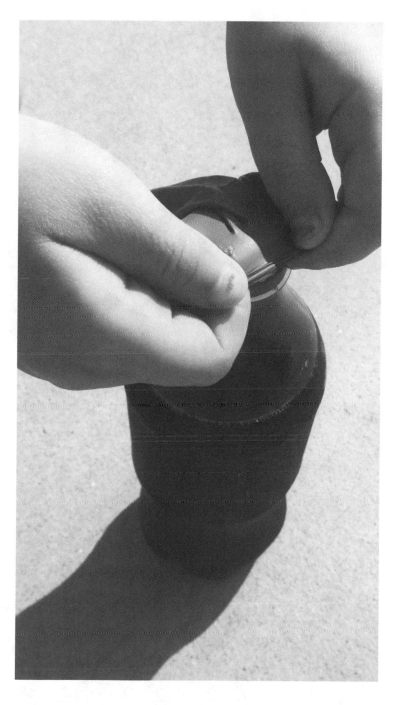

Step 4: Lift the balloon up and let the salt fall into the bottle. Don't be surprised—the balloon will start filling up with gas immediately.

Step 5: Watch the balloon inflate. You might want to support the bottle with your hand to keep it from falling over as the balloon fills up with gas. If it does fall, you can stand it back up. Once the balloon has stopped inflating, take off the balloon and clean up. Taste the soda if you dare. It is completely safe, but it will taste like nasty, flat, salty soda. Normally, you should never taste a chemistry experiment, but this one is completely safe . . . just nasty tasting.

The Science Behind It

You probably already know that sodas are full of carbon dioxide. The carbon dioxide gives the soda the familiar fizz that we love. The carbon dioxide (gas) is actually dissolved in the soda. It can be dissolved in the soda because it is bottled under pressure. When you open a soda, the gas will slowly escape, unless encouraged to escape faster.

In order for a bubble to form, it needs a nucleation point. That point can be an impurity in the bottle—another bubble or a salt (or sugar) crystal. The salt you added created hundreds of nucleation points at the same time, so it created hundreds of bubbles within seconds. This experiment is similar to the Diet Coke and Mentos experiment you may have seen before. The best part of My Soda Has Gas is that it allows you to see how much gas is dissolved in your soda. It is also a little less messy.

Reactions

Chemical reactions are at the heart of how different chemicals combine and how they split apart. Reactions allow atoms to rearrange themselves into new molecules. When chemical reactions occur, new chemicals are formed. Chemists call this a *chemical change*. Chemical changes are not reversible without another chemical change.

Your senses will tell you when a chemical reaction takes place. You will smell a new odor. You will see a solid form from two liquids. You will see and hear bubbles being created as a gas is given off. You will see a color change. You may even feel heat or see light. All of these observations are evidence that a chemical reaction has taken place. Read on and you will learn how to make some safe chemical reactions.

Rubber Egg

Bounce an egg in the name of chemistry.

From the Junk Drawer:

☐ Raw egg
☐ Clear glass
☐ Vinegar
☐ Spoon
☐ Plate or shallow bowl

Step 1: Gently place a raw egg in a clear glass.

Step 2: Fill the glass to about 1 inch above the egg with vinegar.

Step 3: Watch what happens as the egg is in the vinegar. What do you observe? The bubbles indicate a chemical reaction is taking place. It will take about two days to rubberize your egg, so find a place where the glass can remain undisturbed for that long.

Step 4: Remove the Rubber Egg from the vinegar with a spoon. Rinse it off in the sink and place it on a plate or in a shallow bowl.

Step 5: Push your fingertip into it. What does it feel like? You can drop it from few inches onto the plate and watch it try to bounce. You should thoroughly wash your hands when done since Rubber Eggs (and raw eggs) can hang onto some nasty germs.

The Science Behind It

An eggshell is primarily calcium in the form of calcium carbonate. Calcium is the same element that gives you strong bones and teeth. Without calcium, you would be like the Rubber Egg.

The calcium reacts with the acetic acid (vinegar) to dissolve the shell. The white part of the egg becomes the new outside. The membrane of the egg holds the inside together. The membrane is flexible and will break if handled too roughly.

Baby Elephant's Toothpaste

A classic experiment that is safe and fun to play with.

Adult supervision required

From the Junk Drawer:

☐ Outside area

☐ Empty plastic bottle with narrow
   neck

☐ Large baking pan or large pie pan

☐ Hydrogen peroxide

☐ Measuring cup

☐ Dish soap

☐ Food coloring (optional)

☐ Yeast

☐ Spoon

Step 1: You should do this experiment outside, because it will create a big, soapy
mess. Stand an empty plastic bottle up in a baking pan with 2-inch sides
(or similar aluminum pan). Add about ½ cup of hydrogen peroxide to the
empty plastic bottle. A measuring cup makes it easier to pour into the bottle,
but you could pour directly from the hydrogen peroxide bottle. You can use
regular hydrogen peroxide from the medicine cabinet. It is most commonly
sold as a 3 percent solution in almost every store. The reaction will happen
faster (and look a little bit cooler) with 6 percent hydrogen peroxide (called
20-volume hydrogen peroxide), which can be purchased in beauty supply stores.
The pictures below are taken with normal, low-cost 3 percent solution.

Step 2: Add a few drops of dish soap to the bottle. For colored toothpaste, you can add a few drops of food coloring.

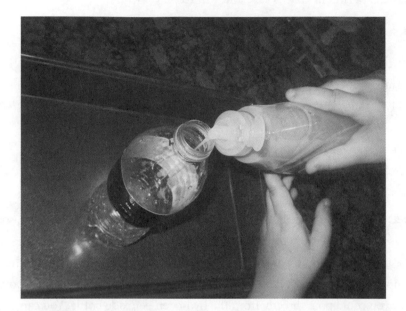

Step 3: Open a dry yeast package and pour it into the measuring cup (or any bowl).

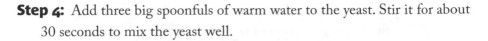

Step 4: Add three big spoonfuls of warm water to the yeast. Stir it for about 30 seconds to mix the yeast well.

Step 5: Pour the yeast mixture into the bottle and watch the reaction.

Step 6: Enjoy the show as the Baby Elephant's Toothpaste just keeps coming out of the bottle. Again, it happens faster with 6 percent solution, but the 3 percent is just as much fun. The foam is safe to play with since it is just oxygen gas and soap. Since you added soap, cleaning up is easy.

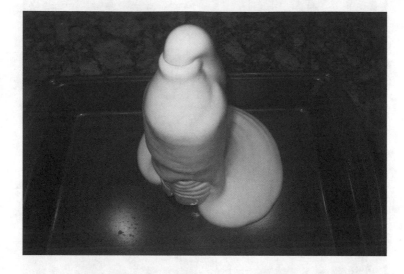

The Science Behind It

Hydrogen peroxide is composed of two hydrogen atoms and two oxygen atoms bonded together. When it decomposes, it breaks down into water and oxygen gas. It will decompose when you pour it onto a surface, such as a cut on your arm. You will notice bubbles created on your cut after adding the hydrogen peroxide. The bubbles are oxygen gas, which helps to kill germs. The leftover water helps to rinse the cut, so hydrogen peroxide is great for treating minor cuts. Hydrogen peroxide will also decompose if exposed to light, so it is always sold in a dark-colored bottle. The decomposition is fairly slow.

Adding soap to the experiment allows you to more easily capture the oxygen bubbles. The yeast acts as a catalyst. Catalysts speed up a chemical reaction. The yeast is a catalyst that causes bubbles of oxygen gas to form faster than they normally would. This experiment is called Baby Elephant's Toothpaste because the foam squeezes out like toothpaste out of a tube. And it takes a lot of toothpaste to brush an elephant's teeth.

Clean Pennies

Make pennies as good as new using chemistry.

From the Junk Drawer:

☐ Dull pennies
☐ Glass or plastic cup (or bowl)
☐ Vinegar
☐ Salt

☐ Paper towels
☐ Water
☐ Packets of soy sauce

Step 1: Place a few dull pennies in a glass or plastic cup. Pour in enough vinegar to cover the pennies. Add a spoonful of salt and stir slightly.

Step 2: Let the pennies sit in the solution for 5 to 10 minutes. Observe what is happening as they sit in the solution. The longer they sit, the cleaner they get. After they are clean, remove the pennies from the solution. Rinse them with water and lay them on a paper towel to dry. Look at how shiny they are now.

Step 3: Rinse out the container with water. Add a few packets of soy sauce to the container and stir in a pinch of salt. Add a few dull pennies and let them sit for 10 minutes. Once the pennies have undergone a physical transformation, pull out the pennies and rinse them off. Compare these pennies to the vinegar pennies.

The Science Behind It

Pennies get dull because the copper on the outside (pennies aren't copper on the inside anymore) reacts with oxygen to form copper oxide. Copper oxide is dull and sometimes even green.

The vinegar/salt solution dissolves the copper oxide off the outside of the penny, exposing shiny copper atoms. Vinegar is a very weak acid, which helps the reaction happen. Soy sauce is also a weak acid, so the same process happens. Cleaning pennies is a great use for those leftover packets of soy sauce that are in your kitchen junk drawer.

> **The only two metals that aren't silver in color are gold and copper.**

Green Pennies

Create colorful pennies and a new chemical at the same time.

From the Junk Drawer:
- ☐ Dull pennies
- ☐ Glass or plastic cup (or bowl)
- ☐ Vinegar
- ☐ Salt
- ☐ Paper towel

Step 1: Repeat step 1 from the previous Clean Pennies experiment (page 129). Place the dull pennies, vinegar, and salt into a glass or plastic cup and let them sit for about 10 minutes.

Step 2: After 10 minutes, remove the pennies. This time, do NOT rinse them. Just put them on a paper towel without drying them. Put the paper towel somewhere to watch what happens. Observe them periodically over the next few hours. Flip the pennies over after they are dry to see even more green.

The Science Behind It

Rinsing the pennies stops the chemical reaction and leaves you with shiny pennies. They will form copper oxide on the outside again, but it will take months. Leaving the salt/vinegar solution on the pennies causes oxides to form on the outside. And it happens very fast.

The blue-green oxide formed on the outside is commonly called *verdigris*. It is a coating often found on metals. It is also formed in minerals that contain copper, giving many copper ores a blue-green color.

Copper Nails

Create copper-coated nails from old, dull pennies.

From the Junk Drawer:

☐ Vinegar

☐ Clear glass or plastic container

☐ Spoon

☐ Salt

☐ 20–25 dull pennies

☐ Steel wool or sandpaper

☐ Iron nails

☐ Paper towels and water

Step 1: Add ¼ cup of white vinegar to a clear container. A glass container will make it easier to see any evidence of the reaction, but plastic works too. Add a spoonful of salt and stir to help the salt dissolve.

Step 2: Slowly drop all of the dull pennies into the solution. Use only dull pennies, since the outside of them is coated with copper oxide. The copper oxide makes the pennies dull in color. Let them sit for 10 minutes and go on to the next step.

Step 3: Use steel wool or sandpaper to clean several iron nails. New nails from the store have a coating on them to prevent them from rusting. The steel wool will take off most of this coating. (The copper will only cover the areas where the coating is rubbed off.) Wipe them down or rinse them off after you finish cleaning them. You are cleaning them to make sure the outside is pure iron. Super silver shiny nails are galvanized with zinc and won't work. Iron nails, when new, are shiny but aren't bright silver in color.

Step 4: Take the pennies out of the solution. You can use a fork, spoon, or your fingers. You will wash everything at the end. Set the pennies on a paper towel to dry. What do you notice about the pennies?

Step 5: Place the clean nail (or nails) in the vinegar and salt solution. You can swirl the container around to speed things up. Leave the nails in for at least 10 minutes, but several hours is better. Now, drain off the solution—it is safe to go down the drain. Rinse off the nails and lay them out to dry. What do you notice? Make sure you wash everything when finished.

The Science Behind It

The acid solution (vinegar) dissolves the copper oxide off the outside of the pennies. The salt helps speed the process up. The copper atoms will stay in the vinegar and salt solution. As you saw earlier, the pennies will come clean after the copper oxide is removed. The copper ions are now positive (because they lost electrons). The copper ions are freely floating in the solution even after the pennies are removed.

The vinegar and salt solution will dissolve some of the iron on the surface of the nail, leaving the nail with a net negative charge. The positive copper ions attach more easily onto the negative nail than the iron ions that dissolved. The positive copper ions will coat the outside of the negative nail until the nail is neutral. You are left with a copper-coated nail.

Coke Non-Float

Create the opposite of a
soda float.

From the Junk Drawer:
☐ Bottle of any brown soda
☐ Milk
☐ Spoon

Step 1: Uncap a bottle of
     cola. (Any brown soda
     will work, even diet
     ones.) Take a small drink
     out of the bottle. Add
     three spoonfuls of milk
     and replace the cap.

Step 2: Put the bottle in a safe place where it won't be disturbed and observe it over the next few hours. What happens? Leave it in a safe place overnight to let the chemical reaction finish.

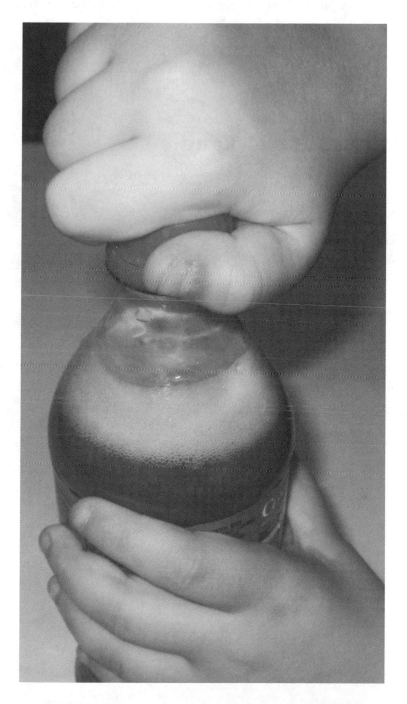

The Science Behind It

The milk molecules combine with the phosphoric acid in the soda to create molecules that are denser than the regular soda molecules. The new heavier molecules then sink to the bottom. The rest of the liquids are less dense and stay near the top. Basically, you have just curdled the small amount of milk with the phosphoric acid in the soda. The curds sink to the bottom and take the color with them.

Emergency Crayon Candle

Light up your house with a crayon.

Adult supervision required

From the Junk Drawer:
☐ Crayon   ☐ Plate
☐ Matches

Step 1: The Emergency Crayon Candle creates more smoke than some candles, so you need to do this experiment in a well-ventilated area. Go to your junk drawer and get a crayon. The crayon must have a wrapper. With adult supervision, light a match. Use the match to melt some of the crayon wax onto a plate. If your crayon has a point, melt the point off, but used, flat-tipped crayons are perfect for this experiment.

Step 2: Blow out the match and immediately stand the crayon up in the puddle of melted wax. The wax will cool quickly, holding the crayon upright.

Step 3: Light another match. Hold the match around the top of the crayon until the wrapper catches on fire. Blow out the match. You have now created an emergency candle.

The Science Behind It

A normal candle is composed of two parts: a wick and paraffin wax. The wick is an absorbent string. Paraffin wax is a compound made up of hydrogen and carbon, like gasoline for your car. When you light the wick, it melts the paraffin wax near the flame. The wax, after it becomes a liquid, is drawn up the absorbent wick. The wax vapor is what burns. The candle is a simple combustion reaction.

A combustion reaction happens anytime you burn a hydrocarbon, like gasoline or paraffin wax. As you probably already know, it takes oxygen gas to keep a fire burning. Some of the oxygen combines with the carbon to form carbon dioxide. Some of the oxygen also combines with the hydrogen to form water. All combustion reactions give off carbon dioxide and water vapor (steam). Other products may also be given off, depending on the purity of the candle wax.

The Emergency Crayon Candle works almost exactly the same way. The wrapper of the crayon burns and vaporizes the wax of the crayon. The vaporized wax contributes to the flame. The flame is larger because the wrapper is paper and paper burns more easily than the wick of a candle. It is important to do this experiment in a well-ventilated area because crayons also contain pigments and other impurities, and the wrapper burns. Blow out the candle before it melts all the way down.

Candle clocks were a common way to keep time a thousand years ago. The candle burns at a regular rate so it can act as a crude clock.

5

Acids and Bases

Acids and bases are special compounds that control a good chunk of our life. Stomach acid helps you break down food for digestion. Acids can also taste good, like orange juice and sodas. Bases are used for cleaning, like soap and shampoo. Acids and bases are almost opposites of each other. Extra stomach acid is neutralized by adding a base like Rolaids, Tums, or Pepto-Bismol. Strong acids and strong bases are both dangerous, but weak acids and bases are used every day. The experiments in this chapter will use some common weak acids and bases, but treat them carefully, for practice. Safety first—always.

Baking Soda Is the Bomb

Go outside and blow up a bag.

Adult supervision required

From the Junk Drawer:

☐ Outside area
☐ Small zippered-style plastic bag
☐ Toilet paper
☐ Baking soda
☐ Spoon
☐ Vinegar
☐ Measuring cup

Step 1: You need a safe, easy-to-clean outside area. A sidewalk or picnic table works well. (You could also do it inside a shower with parental permission.) You need a leak proof bag—the zippered style seals the best. A used sandwich bag is fine; just rinse it out and check for leaks. You can check for leaks by adding water and turning it upside down. Smaller snack-sized bags will also work, but you will just need to cut the amounts in steps 3 and 5 in half. Take four squares of toilet paper and double them over as shown. You will create a rectangle that is two squares long and two squares thick.

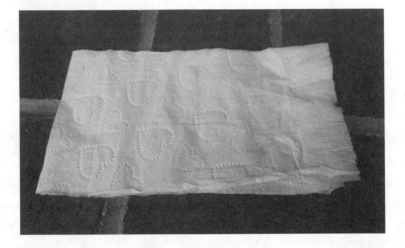

Step 2: Put two spoonfuls of baking soda in a line along the middle of the toilet paper rectangle.

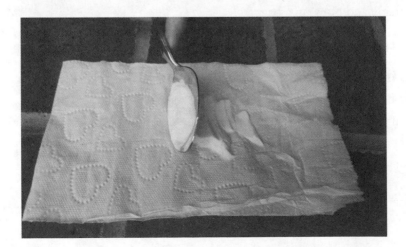

Step 3: Fold the top of the rectangle over and twist up the ends. Twist them up tight, but be careful not to tear the toilet paper. Set aside.

Step 4: Pour ½ cup of vinegar into the zippered sandwich bag.

Step 5: Hold the bag upright on your surface with one hand. Put the baking soda–toilet paper combination into the bag but hold it by pinching the bag so it doesn't touch the vinegar right away. Close the bag with the other hand.

Step 6: Shake the bag a few times and set it down. Stand back and watch it grow and grow. What happened? You can repeat with new bags, varying the amounts of the ingredients. Clean up when you are done and wash your hands.

The Science Behind It

Vinegar is a solution of acetic acid and water. Acetic acid is a weak acid compared to stomach acid or even lemon juice. Baking soda is the chemical sodium bicarbonate, and it is a weak base. Acids and bases neutralize each other by giving off water and a type of salt and sometimes other products. The term *salt* in chemistry is given to the leftover compound in any acid-base neutralization reaction.

The other product in this reaction is carbon dioxide . . . and lots of it. As the carbon dioxide builds up in the bag, it creates more and more pressure. When the inside pressure exceeds the strength of the bag—POW!

Helium was discovered in the sun before it was found on Earth. It was actually named helium after the name for the Greek god of the sun, Helios. It was discovered during a solar eclipse in 1868, when two separate scientists detected a bright yellow spectral line while observing the edge of the sun. It wasn't discovered on Earth until 1895.

Three-Penny Battery

Create your own battery using items from your family's junk drawer.

Adult supervision required

From the Junk Drawer:

☐ Galvanized zinc washers
☐ Scrap of corrugated cardboard
☐ Pen
☐ Scissors
☐ Vinegar
☐ Jar or plastic cup
☐ At least 3 pennies
☐ LED lightbulb
☐ Electrical tape
☐ Wire stripper (optional)

Step 1: Lay a galvanized zinc washer on top of cardboard and trace around it. Repeat to create at least six cardboard circles. Zinc washers are the most common type found. Zinc is bright, shiny, and silver colored.

Step 2: Use scissors to cut out the cardboard disks.

Step 3: Pour about an inch of vinegar into your jar or plastic cup. Soak the cardboard disks in vinegar. Press down on the disks with a pen to submerge them completely. They should stay in the solution for at least one minute.

Step 4: Lay a washer down on a countertop.

Step 5: Take one of the cardboard disks out of the vinegar. Shake off any excess vinegar. Stack it on top of the washer.

Step 6: Place a penny on top of the cardboard disk. The zinc-cardboard-copper combination you just created is called a *cell*. It will deliver less than 1 volt, so you will need more cells to light an LED bulb.

Step 7: Put another washer directly on top of the penny.

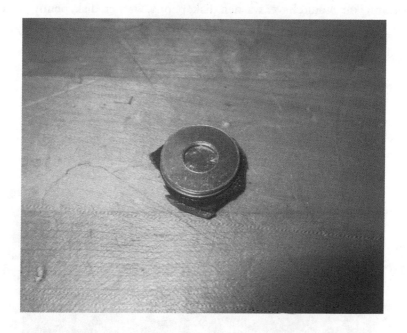

Step 8: Add another cardboard disk. Again, shake off any excess vinegar. The disk should be soaked, but you want to avoid any drips.

Step 9: Put another penny on top and repeat the pattern again. From top to bottom, you should have: washer, disk, penny, washer, disk, penny, washer, disk, penny. This creates a battery with three cells, which will be enough to light an LED bulb.

Step 10: Wrap a piece of electrical tape around the battery to hold it together.

Step 11: You will need an LED light to show off your battery. You can buy them, but there are other sources, like your junk drawer. Old toys that have an LED light will work. Or a string of LED holiday lights that is headed for the trash. When holiday lights go out, usually only one bulb is burned out, but the rest are good. (You can also test the LED with a normal battery to make sure the LED is good.) Almost all portable lights in devices today are LEDs. When you remove the light, keep as much wire as possible. You might want to get adult help to strip some of the insulation off the last ½ inch of each wire. Use scissors (or wire strippers) to lightly cut through the insulation only. Twist the wire as you lightly cut and then pull the plastic insulation off. Stripping wires takes practice, so don't worry if it takes you a few tries. Slide each wire of the LED under the tape on each end of your battery. The LED should light. You can squeeze the wires onto the metals with your hands. The electric current is not strong enough to hurt you, and besides, it would rather go through the metal of the wires instead of your skin. If the LED doesn't light, reverse the wires and try it again. Turn off the lights in the room to see the light better.

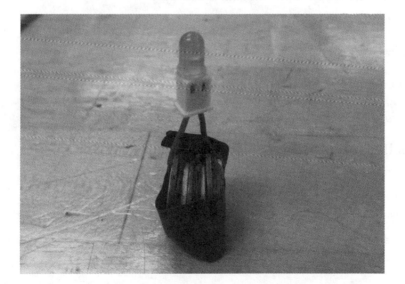

Extensions: Try adding more cells and the bulb will be brighter. You could also try using Gatorade instead of vinegar. Leave the light somewhere safe and see how long your battery lasts.

The Science Behind It

Batteries are created using two different metals with an electrolyte between them. The metals for this experiment were zinc and copper. The electrolyte was the vinegar soaked into the cardboard. The stack with the cardboard between created a cell. The two metals are electrodes. The current will flow from the copper to the zinc. The electrons are free to move through the vinegar and create a current in the electrolyte (vinegar). All acids will act as electrolytes in water.

If you leave batteries in a toy for years, the battery acid will actually leak out and destroy your toy. You have probably seen the remnants of this acid electrolyte if you have opened an old toy with batteries in it.

When you connect the electrodes with any conductor (like the LED and wires) the current will flow through it. LEDs usually take about 1.5 volts to light up. Each cell creates about 0.6 volts. When you stack three cells up, you get 1.8 volts, and the LED will light. More voltage equals a brighter light, but three cells are required to see most LEDs. Experiment and try to create a super bright light from your own homemade battery.

Pour a Gas

Put out a candle flame by pouring an invisible gas on it.

Adult supervision required

From the Junk Drawer:
☐ Measuring cup
☐ Baking soda
☐ Vinegar
☐ Tea light candle
☐ Matches

Step 1: Place a measuring cup on a flat surface for steps 1 and 2. Add about ¼ cup of baking soda to the measuring cup.

Step 2: Slowly add about ¼ cup of vinegar to the measuring cup. You want to add the vinegar slowly so you don't lose any of the gas created. What do you see as it is mixed?

Step 3: With adult permission, light a tea light candle on a surface that is safe for the candle.

Step 4: Lift the measuring cup and tip it so the spout is over the candle. Slowly tip the cup, but *don't pour the liquid out*. You are only going to pour out the invisible *gas*. It may take some practice to get it right, but you can make the flame go out by pouring out the gas.

The Science Behind It

When you mix baking soda and vinegar together a chemical reaction takes place. The bubbles show you that a gas is given off. Chemical reactions almost always create a gas, an odor, or a new color. The gas you created was carbon dioxide. Baking soda is a base, and vinegar is an acid. Whenever you mix an acid and a base together, you create carbon dioxide gas. An acid and a base mixing together is called a *neutralization reaction*.

Carbon dioxide is denser than air, so it will stay inside the measuring cup. When you tip the cup, the gas can pour out onto the candle flame. As you already know, fires need oxygen to burn. Since carbon dioxide is denser than normal air, it will flow to the bottom. With practice you can get the carbon dioxide to stay over the candle for a few seconds. The carbon dioxide blocks oxygen from getting to the candle flame, so the candle goes out.

Bee stings are acidic and wasp stings are basic.

The Self-Inflating Balloon, Type 1

Blow up a balloon in the name of science.

From the Junk Drawer:

☐ Empty plastic drink bottle
☐ Vinegar
☐ Balloon
☐ Funnel
☐ Spoon
☐ Baking soda

Step 1: Rinse out an empty plastic drink bottle and fill it about half full with vinegar.

Step 2: Blow up a balloon and let it deflate several times to stretch it out. Insert a funnel into the neck of the balloon. Put three large spoonfuls of baking soda into the funnel. Stir the baking soda in the funnel to help it get down into the balloon.

Step 3: While letting the balloon hang over the side of the bottle, stretch the neck of the balloon over the top of the bottle, as shown.

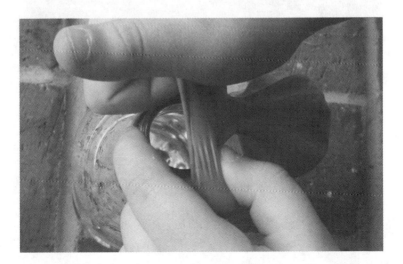

Step 4: Lift the balloon up and let the baking soda fall into the vinegar. You will have to shake the balloon to get all of it to fall in.

Step 5: Stand back and watch the balloon inflate all by itself.

The Science Behind It

This is another version of the classic vinegar–baking soda reaction. The reaction creates carbon dioxide—lots of it. The carbon dioxide inflates the balloon as the pressure builds up. The balloon is stronger than the plastic bag in the previous experiment, so it won't pop. At least I have never had one pop, but you could vary the amounts of baking soda and vinegar and try . . . just be sure to do it outside. Good luck!

The Self-Inflating Balloon, Type 2

Blow up a balloon with a different chemical reaction.

From the Junk Drawer:

☐ Empty plastic drink bottle   ☐ Balloon
☐ Water   ☐ Effervescent tablets

Step 1: Rinse out an empty plastic drink bottle and fill it about half full with water.

Step 2: Blow up a balloon and let it deflate several times to stretch it out. Open a package of effervescent tablets. Alka-Seltzer is a common brand name, but the generic tablets work just as well for this science experiment. Break two tablets into smaller pieces and drop them through the neck of the balloon.

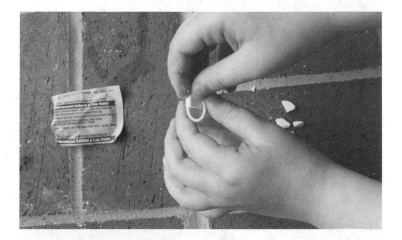

Step 3: While letting the balloon hang over the side of the bottle, stretch the neck of the balloon over the top of the bottle, as shown.

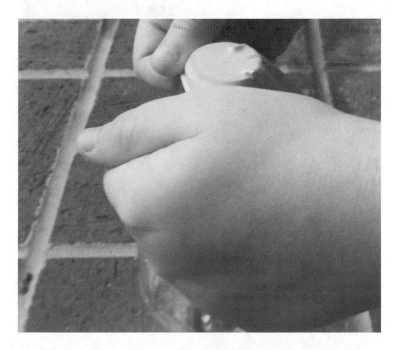

Step 4: Lift the balloon up and let the tablet pieces fall into the water. You will have to shake the balloon to get all of them to fall in.

Step 5: Stand back and watch the balloon inflate all by itself.

The Science Behind It

Most effervescent tablets contain dry citric acid, sodium bicarbonate (baking soda), and aspirin (another weak dry acid). The tablets also contain small amounts of a few other ingredients that will vary between manufacturers, but the citric acid and the baking soda do the fizzy work.

Acids can often be found in a dry condition. They don't behave like acids until they are placed in water. When the dry citric acid dissolves in water, it behaves just like the vinegar in the previous experiment. The citric acid mixes with the baking soda to create even more water, sodium citrate, and carbon dioxide. The carbon dioxide blows up the balloon. The leftover sodium citrate is dissolved in the water. When you drink the sodium citrate solution, it helps neutralize excess stomach acid and you feel better. Sodium citrate is a weak base, so it can neutralize your stomach acid. The aspirin is also a weak acid called acetylsalicylic acid. The aspirin works as an analgesic to reduce pain to further help you feel better.

A gas being produced is a clear sign that a chemical reaction has taken place. Anytime you see bubbles being created, you are witnessing a chemical reaction. If you put hydrogen peroxide on a cut it bubbles. You are watching a chemical reaction. You cut into a birthday cake and see air pockets. These air pockets are bubbles that were baked into the cake as it underwent a chemical reaction in the baking process. Bubbles equal gas, and gas equals chemical reactions. A neutralization reaction is just a special type of reaction between an acid and a base.

Are You Feeling Hot, Hot, Hot?

Learn the secret to speeding up a reaction.

Adult supervision required

From the Junk Drawer:

☐ Effervescent tablet
☐ 3 clear cups
☐ Ice cubes

☐ Water
☐ Scrap paper
☐ Pen or pencil

Step 1: Break an effervescent tablet into three equal-sized portions. Alka-Seltzer is an example of an effervescent tablet, but any brand will do.

Step 2: Fill one cup with water and add an ice cube or two. Fill another cup with room temperature water and let it sit for a few minutes. Fill a third cup with the hottest water you can get from your faucet. Be careful not to burn yourself with the hot water. Put the three cups on a piece of scrap paper and label the cups hot, room temperature and cold.

Step 3: Drop your tablet pieces into each cup as quickly as possible. You can drop them simultaneously if you have a helper. Observe what happens. Which one fizzes the most? Which one fizzes the least? You can also observe which glass completes the fizzing first.

The Science Behind It

If you look at the ingredients on the box your tablet came in, you will see that the tablet contained the following ingredients: an acid (usually citric acid), sodium bicarbonate (baking soda), and usually aspirin. There are also some other lesser ingredients. In tablet form, the acid and the base aren't moving around enough to react. When the tablet is added to water, the acid and the base dissolve and react to form water, a type of salt, and carbon dioxide gas. The carbon dioxide accounts for the bubbles.

The faster the molecules are moving, the faster the reaction takes place. The hot water allows the reaction to occur faster. The hot water also allows the tablet to dissolve faster. Both reasons help the fizz occur quicker.

Chemist Joseph Priestley isolated a vegetable gum that would rub out pencil marks in 1770. Edward Naime, an English engineer, discovered rubber gum at the same time. The eraser was born! An eraser is stickier than the paper on which you've written. Bits of graphite that used to be on the paper would rather stick to the eraser. Before pencil erasers, people often used bread pieces to remove graphite.

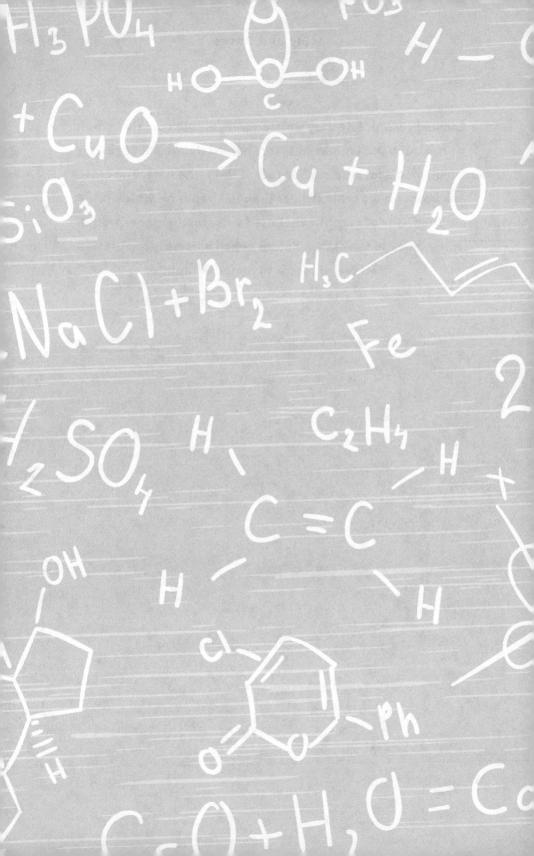

Radioactivity and Thermodynamics

Radioactivity is the process of atoms changing into new atoms. Think of it like a seed growing into a flower. But radioactivity can be dangerous. This chapter contains a few simple and safe experiments to teach you about radioactivity.

This chapter also delves into the wonderful world of heat. Heat is the energy that results from molecules moving. And molecules never stop. They don't take a lunch break, and they don't sit and watch television. All they do is go, go, go. The moving molecules also provide options for a ton of fun experiments.

Chain Reaction

Learn the secret to nuclear power.

From the Junk Drawer:

☐ Dominoes
☐ Pencil
☐ Paper clip boxes or blocks

Step 1: Line the dominoes up as shown in a triangular pattern. Now tip the first domino over and watch what happens. This represents an *uncontrolled chain reaction*. This is what happens when an atomic bomb is exploded.

Step 2: Now stand the dominoes up again as shown. Slide the pencil in near the top of the dominoes and hold it tightly as shown. Tip the first domino over and watch what happens now. This is what happens when you control the chain reaction. You are stopping some of the dominoes from falling.

Step 3: Set up the dominoes again. Now place paper clip boxes (or toy blocks) between the rows of dominoes. Leave the end two dominoes free to fall, but block the rest. Now tip the first domino. You have now completed a *controlled chain reaction*.

Extension: After standing the dominoes up again, experiment with trying to have a controlled chain reaction with a continuous line of three dominoes falling.

The Science Behind It

Nuclear fission is when a large, unstable atom splits into smaller atoms. When this happens, part of the energy holding the large nucleus together is given off as heat. This heat energy can be used to generate electricity. The heat boils water and creates steam, and the steam spins a generator to make electricity. Approximately 20 percent of the United States' electricity is created using nuclear fission.

To start nuclear fission, nuclear engineers shoot a neutron into the large nucleus, which starts the chain reaction. In addition to the heat energy given off, the first atom splitting will release three more neutrons to split other atoms. The number of atoms split increases rapidly. The first split atom creates 3 split atoms, then 9 atoms, then 27 atoms, and so on, and the number grows very fast. This is what you did in step 1.

The uncontrolled chain reaction of an atomic bomb creates an incredible amount of heat all at once. But inside a nuclear reactor, control rods capture some of the extra neutrons and "control" the reaction. By controlling the reaction, the heat released is controlled to make electricity. This is what you did in step 2 with the pencil. The pencil acted as a control rod to stop emitted neutrons from splitting other atoms. To completely control the number of atoms split, you need multiple control rods, as in step 3. The paper clip boxes (or blocks) acted as control rods.

Fission reactors have to be carefully watched by trained engineers to keep them safe. A nuclear reactor is built with the control rods in place, to keep an uncontrolled chain reaction from occurring. To start the process, engineers slowly remove the control rods and a chain reaction begins giving off heat. If they want the chain reaction to stop, the rods are pushed all the way back in.

Fission reactors do have a major danger even if carefully monitored. The leftover smaller atoms are dangerous to be around. They emit dangerous invisible particles that can cause severe damage. The leftover atoms have to be stored safely from people for thousands of years. That is not easy. Think back to when you tried to hide something from someone else. It isn't easy to find a safe hiding place.

Candy Half-Life

Use candy to learn about radioactive atoms.

From the Junk Drawer:

☐ M&M'S candy

☐ Paper towel

☐ Paper

☐ Pencil

☐ Plastic cup

Note: You can also do this same experiment with pennies, but M&M'S taste better.

Step 1: This experiment can be done with any number of candies over 20. (You probably want to do this experiment on a paper towel to keep the candies clean . . . so you can eat them when you're done.) Count the number of M&M'S you start with. Check that the candies actually have a letter on one side. Create a chart on your paper. Label one column Half-Life Shake and the other column Good Atoms. Under Half-Life Shake, write the numbers from 0 to 10. Under Good Atoms, the "undecayed" atoms, write the number of candies you're starting with (see chart on next page).

Half-Life Shake	Good Atoms
0	20
1	
2	
3	
...	

Step 2: Place all of the candies inside a plastic cup. Shake the cup three times and pour out the candies on the paper towel.

Step 3: Gently smooth the candies out so they form a flat layer. Candies with the letter up are considered undecayed "good" atoms and should be pushed into a pile with other undecayed atoms. Dispose of—eat—all of the "decayed atoms," the ones with the letters facing down.

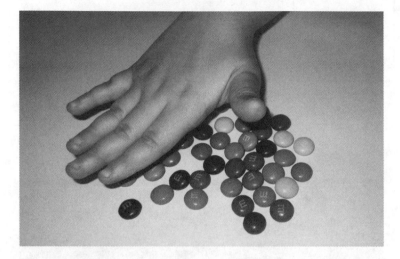

Step 4: Count the number of undecayed atoms and write that number down next to Half-Life Shake 1 on your chart. Place all the undecayed atoms back in the cup.

Step 5: Shake the cup and repeat steps 3 and 4. Remember to record the number of undecayed atoms each time on your chart. Continue repeating steps 3 and 4 until all the undecayed atoms are gone. Add more Half-Life Shake candies if you need to.

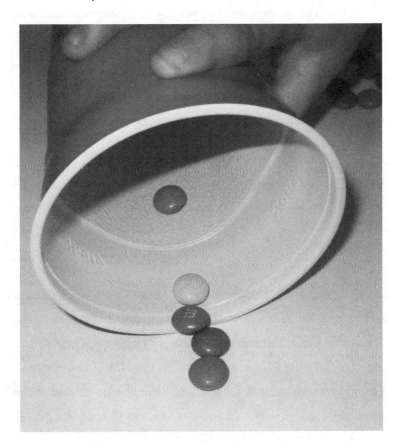

The Science Behind It

Many large atoms are unstable. Unstable atoms are called *radioactive* atoms. These radioactive atoms will naturally give off a radioactive particle (either alpha, beta, or gamma). When they give off this particle, they become more stable. These radioactive particles are invisible and dangerous. Many of the large atoms, like uranium and plutonium, have radioactive isotopes. An isotope is a type of the element that has a different number of neutrons.

Whether a radioactive atom gives off a particle is random, just like whether a candy lands letter side up or down when dropped. With each shake of the cup, about half of your candy atoms "decayed" into new atoms. In nature, these decayed atoms can be new elements. Radioactive uranium will eventually turn into lead, but it takes thousands of years. The time it takes half a sample to change is called *half-life*. Your half-life was each shake of the cup.

In real life, half-lives are different for each radioactive element. The half-life of any radioactive material is measured by scientists and available in books and online. Uranium 235, used in many nuclear reactors, has a half-life of 700 million years. Imagine waiting 700 million years between shakes of your cup. Radioactive iodine, used in medicine, has a half-life of only eight days.

Scientists create graphs out of charts like the one you created. You can create one of your data if you want. Scientists put atoms up the side and time in years across the bottom. Your graph would have the number of shakes across the bottom.

Marie Curie shared the Nobel Prize in 1903 with her husband, Pierre, and Henri Becquerel for her work with radioactivity, but she almost didn't. The French Academy of Science nominated only Pierre and Henri to the Nobel committee. When Pierre found out, he insisted that she be added to the nomination. She was added, and the trio shared the prize.

Coin Dance

Use a glass bottle to make a coin get up and move.

From the Junk Drawer:

☐ Bowl
☐ Ice
☐ Water
☐ Glass bottle
☐ Coin (must be larger than bottle opening)

Step 1: Put some ice and water in a bowl and make sure you have plenty of liquid. Invert a glass bottle in your hand and place the opening of the bottle in the bowl of ice water. With the other hand, place the coin in the cold water.

Step 2: After about a minute, place the bottle upright on a countertop. Place the wet coin over the opening on the top of the bottle.

Step 3: Wrap both of your hands around the bottle. Cover up as much of the bottle as possible. Observe what happens. Also listen for any sounds you hear. Keep your hands there and see how many times you can make the coin dance.

Extension: Try using different coins. Have fun and share this experiment with others. You can also make the coin dance faster if you and a friend both wrap your hands around the bottle at the same time.

The Science Behind It

The experiment begins with a cold bottle filled with cold air. Your hands add heat to the bottle and warm up the air inside. Hot air expands. The water on the wet coin seals the top so the air cannot escape. As the air warms inside the bottle it tries to expand, and the pressure of the air increases. The pressure from the expanding air soon becomes large enough to cause the coin to "burp" out a little warm air.

You can also do this experiment without the ice; simply wet the coin and try the experiment again. The ice speeds up the process by cooling the air first. Since the air is cooler, heat is transferred faster and the coin dances quicker.

Wiggle, Wiggle, Wiggle

Learn the secret to the wiggling atoms in all stuff.

From the Junk Drawer:

☐ Ice tray or shallow plastic container ☐ Water

☐ Freezer ☐ Food coloring

Step 1: Fill up an ice tray and put it in the freezer overnight. If you don't have an ice tray, add water to a plastic container. Put it in the freezer overnight so the water freezes completely. The next morning, add one drop of food coloring to a few of the ice cubes in the tray. Add seven or eight drops if you used a larger plastic container. Put the tray or container back in the freezer. Observe the ice each day for three days. Keep track of your observations each day. After the third day, pop the ice out of its container and look at all sides of the ice. What do you see? Where does the food coloring show up? Does that surprise you?

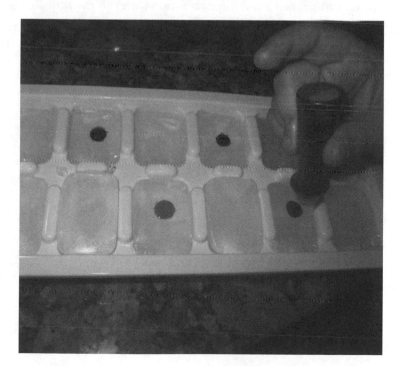

The Science Behind It

One of the fundamental theories of chemistry is the *kinetic molecular theory*. The theory says that molecules in all materials are always moving. They only completely stop at a theoretical temperature called *absolute zero*. Scientists have never gotten to this temperature. It is more than 450 degrees below zero on the Fahrenheit scale!

It is easy to observe the motion of a liquid and a gas. Gas molecules are free to fly around the room. Liquid molecules flow and take the shape of their container. This experiment allows you to see evidence of the solid molecules moving. Molecules in a solid are allowed to wiggle, but they don't travel around. The wiggling of the ice molecules allows the food coloring to move into the piece of ice. Touch a tabletop. The molecules are actually moving. But they are so tiny, when one molecule moves up, the molecule next to it is moving down. Our hand feels it as smooth even though the molecules are wiggling. Of course, the molecules in our fingertip are also wiggling.

The amount of movement is related to the type of material and temperature. Water can be seen in all three common states all the time. Ice is the coldest, and its molecules move the least—they only wiggle. Liquid water is warmer and the molecules can slide. Steam is the hottest and the molecules zoom across the room.

Do-It-Yourself Slushie

Make your own frozen treat.

From the Junk Drawer:

☐ Small zippered-style plastic bag
☐ Juice
☐ Large zippered-style freezer bag
☐ Ice
☐ Salt

☐ Towel
☐ Sink
☐ Spoon
☐ Bowl or tall cup (optional)

Step 1: Pour some juice into a small zippered-style plastic bag with no leaks. A used sandwich bag is fine as long as it is rinsed out and does not leak. Hold it upright and squeeze out all the air as you zip it completely. Freezer bags are a good choice, if you have them, because they are thicker.

Step 2: Put the small bag inside a large zippered bag. Add ice to the large bag.

Step 3: Add salt to the ice in the large zippered plastic bag. About ¼ cup is a good amount, but you don't have to measure it exactly.

Step 4: Seal the large bag. Wrap it in a towel. Massage it with your hands for about 10 minutes. Be careful not to push too hard or the bags may break.

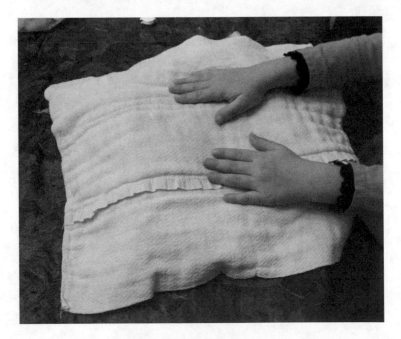

Step 5: After 10 minutes, open the large bag. Take out the small bag. Leave it sealed. Wash it off under the sink with cold water and towel it off well. You want to remove the excess salt and water—a salty slushie does not taste good.

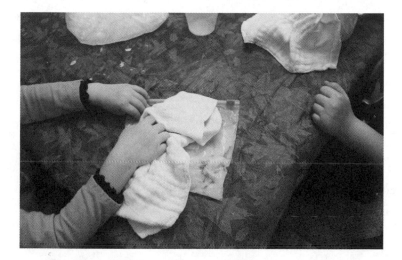

Step 6: Open the bag, grab a spoon, and taste the Do-It-Yourself Slushie. Offer clean spoons to friends and let them dig in. You can pour it all into a bowl or tall cup if you want.

The Science Behind It

The key to this experiment is adding the salt. Heat always flows from hot to cold. The ice is colder than the juice, so heat leaves the juice and starts to melt the ice. When you add salt to the ice, the freezing point of the ice water mixture is lowered. Since the ice and saltwater mixture is now colder, even more heat leaves the juice. The water in the juice begins to freeze as it loses more heat. The frozen water molecules in the juice are what creates the Do-It-Yourself Slushie.

Adding salt to ice is the same scientific process used when creating homemade ice cream. Adding salt to water is also useful to help keep the roads from icing up on cold nights. The salt lowers the freezing point of water. The water on the road will not freeze until it reaches a colder temperature. This makes the streets safer to drive on. Adding salt to the ice also makes the juice in your slushie freeze more quickly.

The lighter was invented before the match.

Cloud in a Bottle

Make a cloud disappear as fast as you create it.

Adult supervision required

From the Junk Drawer:

☐ Thin plastic water bottle with cap
☐ Water
☐ Match

Step 1: Pour a tiny bit of water into a thin plastic bottle (most water bottles today are made very thin to save money and plastic). You only need enough water to just barely cover the bottom. Swirl the water around.

Step 2: Read this entire step before you do it, because it contains two parts that must be done quickly. With adult supervision, light a match. Once it is burning well, drop it into the plastic bottle. The water will put the match out. Immediately cap the bottle so you capture the smoke.

Step 3: Squeeze the bottle as hard as you can. What happens? Now let go of the bottle and observe what happens. Repeat several times. When you are done, rinse out the bottle, dispose of the match, and recycle the bottle.

The Science Behind It

Water vapor is everywhere around us, but we can't always see it. But we do see water vapor when it condenses and turns into liquid around dust particles in a cloud. Clouds are a mixture of dust particles and water vapor. The dust particles give the water vapor something to condense on when the temperature drops. Dust, water vapor, and a falling temperature are all you need.

The Cloud in a Bottle has all three things needed for a cloud. The water vapor comes from the water you added. The smoke from the burning match is like the dust particles. And you created the falling temperature by squeezing and releasing the bottle. When you squeeze the bottle, the pressure and temperature increase. As you release the bottle, the pressure and temperature both fall. The falling temperature causes the water vapor to condense on the smoke particles and you have a Cloud in a Bottle.

The Incredible Soap Monster

Watch a bar of soap grow right before your very eyes!

Adult supervision required

From the Junk Drawer:

☐ Small bar of hotel soap

☐ Plate

☐ Microwave oven

☐ Hot pad

☐ Marker (optional)

Step 1: Ask a parent's permission to use the microwave oven. Unwrap a bar of hotel soap and place it on the center of a plate. Almost all soap bars will work, but this is a perfect use for the tiny bars of soap you get from hotels. You can even do this at the hotel if it has a microwave oven.

Step 2: Place the plate inside the microwave oven and microwave on high for two minutes. You will do no harm to the soap, microwave, or plate. Depending on the power of your microwave, the soap should reach full size before two minutes. If you microwave it longer, it will probably begin to shrink.

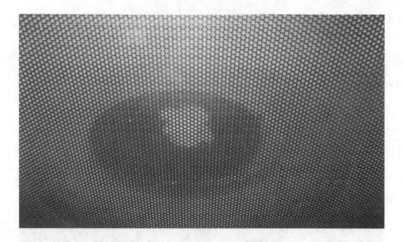

Step 3: Use a hot pad to remove the plate from the microwave oven and inspect your Incredible Soap Monster. Let it cool for at least two minutes before you attempt to touch it. It is still regular soap and can still be used.

Extension: Draw a face on a new bar of soap with a marker before you put it in the microwave and try the experiment again.

The Science Behind It

As it grows, the soap is undergoing a *physical change*, like breaking a piece of chalk. A physical change does not create anything new. A *chemical change* (like the ones you created in chapter 4) creates a new substance.

Two things happen to the soap bar in the microwave. One, the soap itself heats up and softens. And two, the tiny bubbles of air trapped inside the soap bar heat up. This causes water vapor in the bubbles to vaporize and expand. Since the bubbles grow, the Incredible Soap Monster grows as well. The soap hasn't changed except in size, and it is a little more flakey. Use it in your next bath or shower and you will still come out as clean as ever.

Can Crusher

Crush a can in the name of science.

Adult supervision required

From the Junk Drawer:

☐ Empty aluminum soda can
☐ Water
☐ Spoon
☐ Stove top

☐ Large mixing bowl
☐ Ice
☐ Cooking tongs or hot pad

Step 1: You will need adult help for this experiment, and the payoff is worth it. Put two or three spoonfuls of water in a rinsed out, empty aluminum soda can. With adult help, place the can on your stove top with the opening facing up and turn the heat to **medium**. Let the can heat up for about two minutes. Do not use high heat.

Step 2: Fill a large mixing bowl about halfway with water. Add at least a dozen ice cubes. The more ice cubes you add, the neater the experiment. The mixing bowl should be safe on a kitchen counter next to the stove top.

Step 3: The can will be hot, so **do not touch it without the tongs or a hot pad**. Grasp the can with the tongs.

Step 4: Quickly turn the can upside down and put the opening in the ice water bath. Let go of the can. **Make sure you turn off the stove top.**

Step 5: Pick the can up again with your tongs. Water comes pouring out! But didn't the can only have a tiny bit of water?

The Science Behind It

At room temperature, the air pressure inside the can is equal to the air pressure outside the can, so the wall of the can is stationary. (Air pressure is the result of air molecules colliding with a surface.) Even as the can heats, the air pressure is equal, so the wall doesn't move. As the can heats, the water you put in the can will turn into water vapor, which pushes the air molecules out of the can.

When you invert the can and dunk it into the ice water, there is a rapid change in pressure as the gaseous water vapor molecules turn back into a liquid. The liquid water takes up much less room that the hot gaseous water vapor. The void created by the water vapor as it changes back into a liquid creates very low pressure inside the can. The air pressure outside is still normal air pressure, much higher than the inside pressure. The outside air pressure wins and crushes the can inward. The outside air pressure also pushes water up into the can. Air pressure is powerful!

A television set can run for more than three hours on the energy saved from recycling one aluminum can.

Homemade Shrinky Dinks

Watch your artwork shrink into tiny masterpieces.

Adult supervision required

From the Junk Drawer:

- ☐ Scrap of #6 recyclable plastic
- ☐ Scissors or serrated knife
- ☐ Permanent markers
- ☐ Access to a concrete sidewalk (optional)
- ☐ Oven
- ☐ Cookie sheet
- ☐ Parchment paper or aluminum foil
- ☐ Hot pad
- ☐ Metal pan

Step 1: Dig through your recycling bin to find some #6 recyclable plastic containers. (Note: not all recycling programs take #6 plastic, but many do.) Look for the triangular recycling logo—#6 plastic is commonly used in meat trays, salad bar containers, and bakery item containers, as well as for recyclable plastic drink cups. Only #6 plastic works for this project. With adult permission, use scissors to cut flat pieces out of the plastic containers.

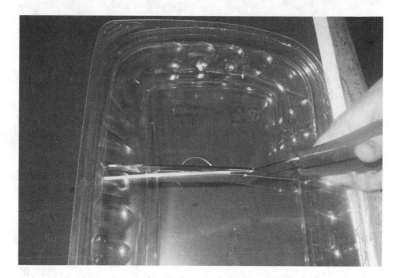

Step 2: For plastic cups, with adult help, use a serrated knife to cut the bottom of the cup off. The sides can be shrunk also, but they will curl up too fast and are not suitable for artwork.

Step 3: For larger groups, like a classroom or a birthday party, have an adult cut a small slice through the bottom side of multiple cups. You can then use scissors without adult help to trim the bottoms off.

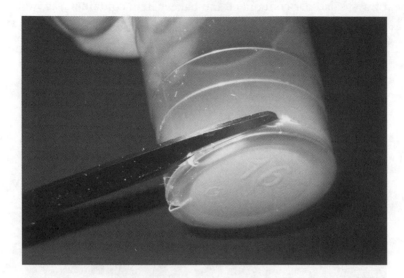

Step 4: Use scissors to trim the bottom until you have any desired shape, like a circle, a square, or a triangle. You can use the point of a pair of scissors to create a hole if you want to make a charm for a necklace. Make the hole *before* you bake your shrinky dink.

Step 5: You are now ready to create your masterpieces. For a fun option, rub your plastic back and forth on a concrete sidewalk. This scratches the plastic and makes it look like frosted glass. It will look great either way; the frosted look adds variety to your artwork.

Step 6: Use permanent markers to draw on the plastic. You can draw flowers, houses, or anything you want. Be creative and use lots of colors if you have them—the colors will stay when the plastic shrinks. You can also write your name, the name of your favorite book, or any saying you want.

Step 7: If your plastic container has a design stamped into the plastic, color the lines or the flat part of the design to create a really cool art project.

Step 8: With adult help, heat the oven to 350 degrees Fahrenheit. Spread a piece of parchment paper or aluminum foil on a cookie sheet. Lay all of your artwork on the cookie sheet. **Do not put any plastics other than #6 in the oven, ever.**

Step 9: Turn the light on in your oven so you can watch. Place the cookie sheet on the oven rack. The shrinking will start to take place within two minutes and will be done before five minutes is up.

Step 10: The plastic may curl up as it shrinks, and this is normal. If it curls too much, have an adult take it out of the oven and push it down with a metal pan. **DO NOT touch the plastic**, as it will be very hot for about two minutes. If the plastic is not done shrinking, put it back in the oven for a few more minutes. If a piece curls up and touches itself, it will melt together and you won't be able to save it. It is always a good idea to make extras for this reason. Cup bottoms tend to curl up more than flat pieces.

Step 11: Pull the cookie sheet out of the oven using hot pads and let it cool off. Two or three minutes is enough for your Homemade Shrinky Dinks to cool off, but be careful—**the cookie sheet will stay hot longer.**

Step 12: Admire and show off your artwork. An unshrunk cup bottom is included in the picture to show you that the cup bottoms don't shrink as much as thinner flat pieces, but they still look neat. The cup bottoms are thicker and only shrink to about half of their original diameter. The thinner flat pieces will shrink down to five or six times smaller.

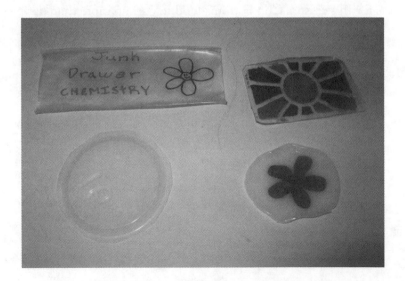

The Science Behind It

Plastic #6 is called *polystyrene*. Raw polystyrene is heated, rolled flat, and cooled very quickly to form the plastic containers used for food. This leaves the polystyrene as a long, straight polymer. But polystyrene is actually a bunched up, curled polymer in its raw form. When you heat #6 plastic without rolling it flat, it changes back to its normal bunched-up polymer. And as this happens the long, straight polymers shrink to a smaller bunched-up polymer. Polystyrene is called a *thermoreactive plastic* because its properties can be changed by heat.

Glossary

acid: a sour solution that will react with a base

air: a mixture of all the gases around us, made up of 78 percent nitrogen, 21 percent oxygen, and 1 percent other types of gas

atom: basic building block of the world around us

attract: when something pulls toward something else

base: a bitter solution that will react with an acid

battery: a device that converts chemical energy into electrical energy

catalyst: a material that speeds up a chemical reaction

chemical change: a change in which a new substance is formed

chemical reaction: interaction of two or more compounds that creates a different compound

chemistry: branch of science dealing with how matter acts by itself and how matter reacts with other matter

chromatography: a method of separating and analyzing chemicals

compound: a combination of elements that always occurs in a set ratio

crystal: a solid having a geometric shape that repeats

density: how tightly compacted a substance is, commonly measured in grams per cubic centimeter

elastic: a material that naturally returns to its original shape after being squeezed or stretched

electrolysis: breaking a chemical compound apart by passing an electric current through it

electrolyte: a solution that conducts electricity

electron: negative subatomic particle, found outside the nucleus in the electron cloud

electron cloud: region around the outside of the nucleus where electrons reside

element: naturally occurring substance; only 92 different ones make up everything in the world

fission: splitting of an atom into two new atoms; releases energy

fluid: any substance, such as a gas or a liquid, that flows

fusion: joining together of two smaller atoms to form a larger atom; releases energy as this happens; powers our sun

gas: state of matter in which the atoms or molecules can take any shape and volume

half-life: the time it takes for one half of a radioactive sample to decay

ion: an atom that has gained or lost electrons and is electrically charged

isotope: an atom of the same element with a different number of neutrons

kinetic molecular theory: the theory that states that atoms are always moving, even when they are in a solid form

liquid: state of matter in which atoms or molecules have a definite volume but can take any shape

molecule: a combination of atoms that is always in a set ratio; for example, two hydrogen atoms and one oxygen atom make a molecule of water

neutralization: chemical reaction in which an acid and a base combine to form a type of salt and water

neutron: neutral subatomic particle that is found in the nucleus of an atom

non-Newtonian fluid: a fluid that changes viscosity based on the force applied to it

nucleus: center, positive part of an atom

periodic table: table that shows all of the elements known to man

plasma: state of matter in which you find an electrically charged gas; commonly found inside fluorescent light tubes and inside the sun

polymer: a long, chain-like structure composed of many smaller molecules

pressure: the force per unit area that is present any time two objects are in contact

proton: positive subatomic particle that is found inside the nucleus of the atom

radioactivity: the emission of particles as a substance's nucleus decays

repel: when something pushes away from something else; positive charges repel positive charges and negative charges repel negative charges

salt: combination of a metal and a nonmetal that is left after a neutralization reaction occurs

solid: state of matter in which the atoms have a definite shape and definite volume

solution: one substance dissolved in another substance

state of matter: one of the four unique forms that matter can take on—solid, liquid, gas, or plasma

surface tension: elastic-like force that is found at the surface of a liquid

temperature: measure of the average kinetic energy of a substance

thermodynamics: branch of science that deals with how heat energy is related to other types of energy

viscosity: measure of the thickness of a fluid

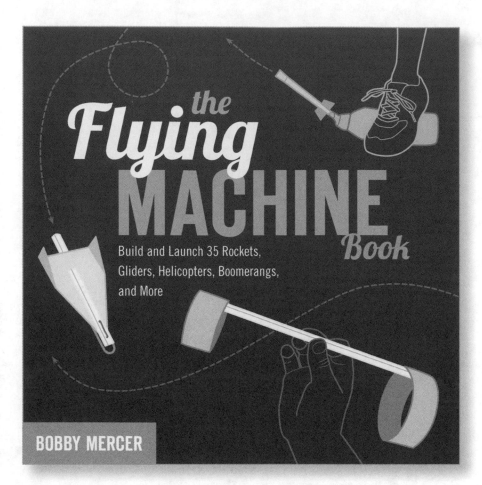

The Flying Machine Book
Build and Launch 35 Rockets, Gliders, Helicopters, Boomerangs, and More
by Bobby Mercer

200 B/W Photos
20 B/W Illustrations

"Hands-on activities that encourage imaginations to soar." —*Kirkus Reviews*

Trade Paper, 208 Pages
ISBN-13: 978-1-61374-086-6
$14.95 (CAN $16.95)
Ages 9 and up

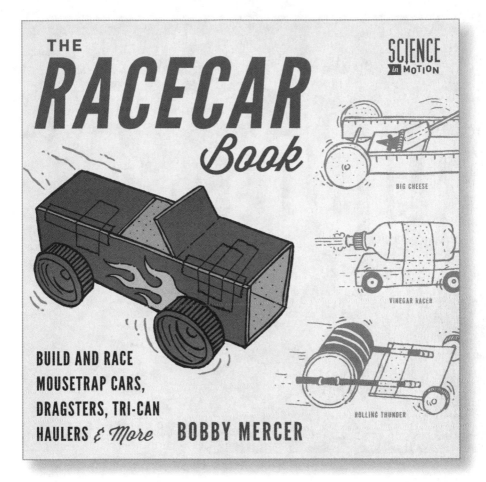

The Racecar Book
Build and Race Mousetrap Cars, Dragsters, Tri-Can Haulers & More
by Bobby Mercer

200 B/W Photos
20 B/W Illustrations

"Highly recommended." —*The Midwest Book Review*

Trade Paper, 216 Pages
ISBN-13: 978-1-61374-714-8
$14.95 (CAN $16.95)
Ages 9 and up

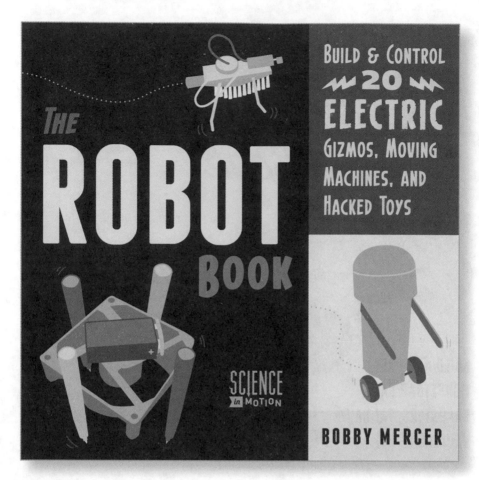

The Robot Book
Build & Control 20 Electric Gizmos, Moving Machines, and Hacked Toys
by Bobby Mercer

200 B/W Illustrations

"Mercer shows readers that by being curious, by observing, and by understanding the basics of machines and electricity, they can make small, amusing robots. Several of the projects don't even require electricity but still offer kids a chance to create something amazing." —*Booklist*

Trade Paper, 208 Pages
ISBN-13: 978-1-55652-407-2
$14.95 (CAN $17.95)
Ages 9 and up

CHICAGO REVIEW PRESS

Available at your favorite bookstore, by calling
(800) 888-4741, or at www.chicagoreviewpress.com